Diplomacy
The Written Art

Diplomacy
The Written Art

Ozichi Alimole

HEBN Publishers Plc

HEBN Publishers Plc

Head Office: 1 Ighodaro Road, Jericho, P.M.B. 5205, Ibadan
Phone: (02) 2412268, 2410943, 2411213; *Fax:* (02) 2411089, 2413237
E-mail: info@hebnpublishers.com
            hebnpublishers@yahoo.com
Website: http://www.hebnpublishers.com

Area Offices and Branches
Abeokuta . Abuja. Akure . Bauchi . Benin City . Calabar . Enugu .Ibadan
Ikeja . Ilorin . Jos . Kano . Katsina . Maiduguri . Makurdi . Minna
Owerri . Port Harcourt . Sokoto . Uyo . Yola . Zaria

ISBN 978 978 081 023 8

Printed by Polygraphics Ventures Limited, Ibadan

Acknowledgements

I wish to acknowledge my debt of gratitude to the following persons whose advice, remarks and motivation helped me in writing this book.

First, my thanks go to His Excellency, Mr. M. U. Offor, Nigeria's Ambassador to Botswana. I visited Ambassador Offor in 2006 during the Seminar of Nigerian Heads of Mission in Asia and the Middle East held at the Nigeria High Commission, India. He was then the Deputy High Commissioner of the Mission. I informed him that I was writing a book on diplomacy but regretted that I hadn't found enough material on the aspect of diplomacy that interested me. Soon after I returned to the Repubic of Singapore   where I was head of Mission, Ambassador Offor sent me three books by former Indian Ambassador and Academic, Professor Krishan S. Rana. I called Ambassador Offor immediately to ask how much I should pay for the books. He merely laughed 'diplomatically' over the question and I understood that he didn't need my money. The books were a gesture to encourage my endeavour. I found Professor Rana's books and Lecture series invaluable especially on the subject of Performance Measurement in Foreign Ministries.

My thanks also go to the Doyens of modern diplomacy literature, notably Sir Ernest Satow, and R. G. Feltham whose works served as resource material for this book. I am also indebted to G.R. Berridge, Charles Freeman, Jan Melissen and Brian Hocking, among others, whose books gave me greater insight into the similarity of challenges facing Foreign Ministries today as they struggle to remain relevant in our communication age.

I am grateful to my former colleagues and friends in the Nigerian Ministry of Foreign Affairs who confessed they'd found value in my previous books on aspects of diplomacy and encouraged me to write more. I thank them all.

I appreciate my elder brother, Mr B.J. Alimole who never ceases to applaud my modest effort in whatever I write such that he has become an inspiration and a challenge.

My thanks go also to my children: Kem, Tonna, Afonne and Ndidi who never stop prodding me to complete the book.

Finally, Chisara, my wife deserves all the credit for being my trusted and impartial critic and motivator. She was the one holding the candle while I did the writing of this book.

Preface

Since the past few decades, there has been a trend towards what diplomacy writers have described as the 'corporatization' of government business or the application of business management principles to the operations of government Ministries and Agencies.

Corporatization is borne out of the growing public interest in the activities of government ministries and departments which are financed with the tax payers' money. Accordingly, Ministers are randomly summoned by the Committees of National Assemblies to either explain or defend the functions of their ministries in the same manner that shareholders summon chief executives of companies to explain the performance of their companies.

This trend which began in the developed countries is rapidly catching on in the developing world. But while most government Ministries and agencies have been quick to modify their operations and structures to achieve the goals of corporatization, the Ministries of Foreign Affairs (MFAs) have not shown equal zeal for change to achieve optimum performance.

Two reasons are believed to account for the apparent resistance of MFAs to change. First is the still unresolved controversy over the status of diplomacy: is it a specialized profession or is the MFA merely another government ministry? Second is the very nature of diplomacy itself: it is primarily a secretive business ironically sets against the need of the citizens' right to know in a democratic setting.

Diplomacy scholars and practitioners have rightly argued that diplomacy is a specialized profession like any other profession and that, beyond consular services, most of the other functions of diplomats are not visible to the general public. Put differently, a greater part of the work of diplomats can neither be quantified nor expressed in a manner that would be meaningful to the public.

Regrettably, this line of argument has, at least in part, provided comfort for Foreign Ministries that have shown little desire to encourage the development of written communication - the critical diplomatic skill that would support the view of diplomacy as a specialized profession.

In a number of developing nations, governments have reacted to the above claims of diplomacy as a profession whose functions are inaccessible to the tax payer in a number of radical ways: in some countries, the role of Foreign Ministries have been downgraded in an important way either through deep and sustained budgetary cuts or the establishment of parallel Ministries to usurp their statutory functions. At other times, staff deployments to and from the Ministries of Foreign Affairs have been effected in a manner to reaffirm the view of governments that perhaps diplomacy is not really a specialized profession after all.

This is a challenge that career diplomats-both serving and retired-cannot afford to ignore if they expect to win the raging silent war against the many fortune hunters who now take up a lion share of diplomatic appointments in most countries. It is, in my view, a matter of relevance and integrity. With improved written communication powers, Foreign Ministries and their diplomats can reach out to the many and ever-growing constituencies that expect them to justify their existence.

This book is an attempt to redefine diplomacy in terms of what it truly is: an art of learning to write in a special way. It is not like journalism. Nor is it like literary studies. Diplomatic writing has its own form, language and mood. It is unlike any other form of written communication. If I may paraphrase an American humorist, it is like the art of telling a man to go to hell in such a manner that he truly looks forward to going there with gladness!

Indeed, the peculiarity of diplomacy communication is perhaps the strongest case in favour of diplomacy as a specialized profession. Ironically, most Foreign Ministries, especially in Anglophone developing countries seem to take the development of this important skill for granted. Diplomacy writers and intellectuals do not seem to have fared better. They have tended to focus on diplomatic history, relations building, protocols, privileges and immunities, etc at the expense of the very critical tool for effective diplomacy: that is, the written communication.

So, *Diplomacy: The Written Art* is an effort to refocus attention on the significance of diplomatic communication as one of the defining characteristics of diplomacy. I have put together in this volume a wide variety of correspondence types that diplomats encounter on a daily basis with a step-by-step analysis of each form of correspondence and suggestions on how Foreign Ministries and their team of Foreign Service Officers can achieve diplomatic excellence. The last part of the book contains important tools to measure performance and promote written communication among Foreign Affairs Officers as the most essential skill of diplomatic practice.

Diplomacy: The Written Art is the outcome of my long experience as a career diplomat spanning over two decades. The book should serve as a training manual in Foreign Service Academies and Institutions as well as a 'student's companion' for all classes of diplomats, including those who would like to choose diplomacy as a career.

Ozichi Alimole
Abuja
February 2008

Contents

Acknowledgements v

Preface vii

Chapter One   Basic Forms of Correspondence 1

Chapter Two   Correspondence with Diplomatic Missions .. 11

Chapter Three   Advanced Correspondence 23

Chapter Four   Common Forms of Presidential
                    Correspondence 27

Chapter Five   Specialized Presidential Correspondence I ... 39

Chapter Six   Specialized Presidential Correspondence II .. 45

Chapter Seven   Specialized Ministerial Correspondence 51

Chapter Eight   Basic Correspondence on Arrival at Post 59

Chapter Nine   Miscellaneous Communication 63

Chapter Ten   Performance Measurement in Diplomatic
                    Systems 73

Chapter Eleven: Concluding Remarks 89

Suggestions for Further Reading 90

Annex I   Vienna Convention on Diplomatic
                    Relations 91

Annex II   Vienna Convention on Consular
                    Relations 109

Annex III   Glossary of Diplomatic Terms 143

Index   155

1

Basic Forms of Correspondence

1.1 Correspondence to Acknowledge Receipt of Letters, etc.

Correspondence to acknowledge the receipt of letters and related communication represents the first major test of the writing skill of young entrants into the Foreign Service of any country. At first, the task may seem easy. But experience has shown that, in fact, it isn't. For this reason, prudent heads of departments usually insist on seeing the draft prepared by their younger subordinates before the letter is 'issued', that is, dispatched.

Elsewhere, I have had occasion to suggest that the quality of correspondence that originates from your desk defines your character, work habit and even intelligence. You may be a smart guy. But if you don't show it by the standard of your written expression, nobody will believe that you are as smart as you think you are.

Besides, your written expression is the mirror through which the general public perceives your organization. If the quality of your writing is poor or lousy, people will tend to have a low opinion of your organization and its personnel. You may adorn the best suits and colorful *agbada*. But you'll lose the respect of the people you are supposed to serve because they would think you don't deserve it. In your presence, they may compliment your smart and flamboyant attire. But in your absence, they'd say, "This guy doesn't know nothing! See the rubbish he's written!"

Now, what makes it so difficult to write good acknowledgement letters?

First, young diplomats may not be fully aware of what it means to acknowledge the receipt correspondence. Let's suppose that your immediate supervisor has sent you a *minute* saying, 'Please acknowledge receipt.' And, depending on the degree of confidence he has in you, he may or may not add, 'Please let me see your draft before you issue the letter.'

For the new entrant into a Foreign Ministry or any other serious organization for that matter, this directive may seem unnecessary. After all, to acknowledge the receipt of a correspondence, it's enough to write simply, 'I am directed to acknowledge the receipt of your ...'

The second is tradition. Young officers are routinely advised to read files' to see 'how we do things.' Regrettably, 'how we do things' may not be the best. Consequently, the young officer is, right from the onset, trapped like an ensnared rat, in an obsolete tradition or habit of doing things. It takes courage to impose one's originality and creativity on a tradition that has survived several generations. For a young officer, this would be almost impossible because, a difficult supervisor would tend to consider the initiative an intolerable rebellion against 'the way we do things.'

The third is nonchalance—an attitude of mind that suggests that, so long as the recipient can understand what you've written, it doesn't really matter how you write it. This is perhaps the most common reason for poor quality of written correspondence everywhere. Officers deny themselves the opportunity to acquire the necessary skill for good writing, believing that one piece of writing is as good as any other!

1.2   Structure of Acknowledgement Letters

We generally tend to think that a letter to acknowledge the receipt of a correspondence is very easy because we are unaware that it has a structure. Indeed, a letter to acknowledge the receipt of a correspondence should have the following parts:

- *Opening*
- *Content*
- *Concluding Statement, and*
- *Signature.*

1.2.1 The Opening

The *Opening* is the place for the common phrase known to Public Officers: "I am directed to ...." Regrettably, most letters to acknowledge the receipt of a correspondence stop at the opening stage. Let's suppose that the Executive Secretary of an International Organization has just forwarded to your Minister the Report of an Election Observer Group to Liberia with a covering letter. As a young officer, you are directed to acknowledge the receipt of the Report.

In most cases—except you are computer literate and the 'miracle machine' is not a luxury in your organization—you would probably grab pen and paper and, off you go:

(a)   *I am directed to acknowledge the receipt of your letter, Reference number EW/77/IX under cover of which you kindly forwarded the Report of the recent Election Observer Group to Liberia.*
Or better still, you may write:

(b)   *I am directed to acknowledge receipt of your letter, Reference No. EW/77/IX, forwarding the Report of the recent Election Observer Group to Liberia.*

The phrase, *under cover of which* is a tongue-twister and somewhat clumsy. For all practical purposes, I would recommend the second variant. It is 'user- friendly', simple and easy to read.

1.2.2 The Content

What about the content of the Report? You may choose your preferred variant, i.e. options (a) or (b). But don't celebrate. The task is not over. You've got to say something about the Report itself to convince the sender that his Report has been read and that it was worth the trouble sending the Report in the first place. You should also indicate what action, if any, your organization has taken or plans to take with regard to the content of the Report.

The above principle has a wider application. For example, when at Headquarters you're required to acknowledge the receipt of a *Chancery Report*, it is hardly enough to write something like this:

"*We wish to acknowledge with thanks the receipt of the Report titled, 'The Persistence of Racial Discrimination and Slavery in Latin America" which you forwarded to us under cover of your letter Reference No. NIG/BRZ/03/IV of 25 May 2003.*

Yours Ever,
Office of the Honourable Minister of Foreign Affairs."

It is important to recognize that the writer of a Chancery *Report* has devoted time and effort to produce it. He or she expects to know your views on the subject matter, and this should be expressed clearly in your acknowledgement letter. So, we should not hesitate to commend the Report and, where appropriate, point to its failings, and suggest ways to improve on future Reports.

As in the previous example, the writer should not be left in any doubt that his Report has received the highest possible attention and that its content is consistent with the national interest of the nation.

1.2.3 The Concluding Statement
A letter to acknowledge the receipt of a correspondence should end with a concluding statement. A concluding statement may indicate, for instance, that the report or correspondence was valuable in a particular sense and that an 'appropriate action' is being taken, or will be taken in due course to give effect to the focus of the Report

1.2.3 The Signature
When we are required to acknowledge the receipt of a correspondence, we do so in some cases on behalf of some superior authority. In most Foreign Ministries, (Department of State in the United States and Foreign and Commonwealth Office in the United Kingdom), the Minister or Secretary of State, as the case may be, is the head of the organization. In those instances, heads of Departments or Divisions or Schedule Officers may sign all out-going correspondence on behalf of the head of the organization, with the word 'for' prefixed to the designation of the head of the organization.

e.g.
Yours Sincerely,

Dr Musa Ojukwu Balogun
Deputy Director (Division of African Studies)
For: Honourable Minister of Foreign Affairs

It does not appear, there are hard and fast rules as to whether an officer signing the correspondence on behalf the Chief of his Organization should or should not state his own official designation. In some cases, the full name of the Schedule Officer will do. But for all practical purposes, it would be desirable that the status of the officer be clearly stated to reflect the degree of importance that the organization attaches to the matter under consideration. Remember: The secretary should leave enough room for signature. This is especially important for those whose signatures are as long as half a page!

1.3   Correspondence to Forward Letters

The act of forwarding letters or documents from an *addresser* to an *addressee* is one of the primary functions of Ministries of Foreign Affairs the world over. Generally, officials of Foreign Ministries consider this task irritating as when, in moments of exasperation, they exclaim, "Damn it! They think we're a mere Post Office!"

I share the view that the degree of commitment of Ministry Officials in matters of forwarding correspondence to its highest destination will, to a large extent, determine whether the general public will think of your Ministry as a glorified Post Office and your Chief Executive, a Post Master General.

Indeed, Foreign Ministries serve as the window of their respective countries to the world. They represent the focal point for foreign individuals, organizations and governments who desire to establish contacts with other countries. Admittedly, some developing countries observe this provision more in violation than adherence. This is especially true of private sector organizations. They would go to any length to cut off the hands and legs of government bureaucracy to achieve narrow corporate objectives.

However, whether by design or by default, Foreign Ministries remain the critical point of contact between governments and organizations that desire to foster healthy and transparent relationships. This function entails the movement of considerable amount of correspondence from one country to the other through the Ministries of Foreign Affairs.

So, how do Foreign Affairs Officials transmit the mass of correspondence that come to their desks? Which are the common types of letters that may come your way in the course of your career?

1.3.1 Correspondence to Forward Sealed Letters

First, letters may arrive in sealed envelopes and usually addressed by one head of state to another. Correspondence to forward letters in sealed envelopes is fairly easy. Your choices are limited because, except you are a magician, you would have no idea what the envelope contains. So, nobody will query you for failure to comment on the substance of the letter. In this case, it would be sufficient to address your *covering letter* to the appropriate authority that has responsibility to receive official mail on behalf of the head of State.

Here is an example:

> *I am directed to forward herewith a sealed envelope addressed to Mr. President by his friend and brother, the President of the Republic of Ghana. Please arrange to place the said envelope before Mr. President at the earliest opportunity.*

You may then request the receiving authority to acknowledge the receipt of your correspondence. Be sure your request for acknowledgement is expressed in a suitable polite format.

1.3.2 Correspondence to Forward Sealed Letters, with Attached Copy

Letters may also arrive in a sealed envelope, but with a copy of the message attached to it. In this case, you have the opportunity to see the content of the message. So, to forward the sealed envelope to its highest destination, you should not be content with merely saying, 'I am directed to forward herewith...' If you stop at that, you may unwittingly be turning your Ministry into a Post Office and your Minister, a Post Master General! Instead, you should try to do the following:

> * *Open your forwarding letter in the traditional style, viz:*
> *I am directed to forward herewith a letter addressed to Mr. President by his colleague and brother, the President of the Republic of ...*

Notice that I have eliminated the word 'sealed envelope.' What's the use of congesting your sentence with words, like in Lagos traffic, when you can safely do without them? In any case, you already have a copy of the message. So, it is immaterial whether the envelope is sealed or open, unless you have good reasons to suspect that the envelope might contain something other than the copy of the message attached to it.

Next, state the opinion of your Organization in relation to the content of the message, bearing in mind the foreign policy of your government or institution.

Suppose that a foreign head of State has invited your President to a Fund Raising dinner and you believe that it would be inappropriate for your President to honour the invitation. In the forwarding letter, you should say so, and if necessary, suggest that your country's ambassador to that country should be asked to represent your Head of State at the event. Be sure to give reasons why your Head of State should not attend the fund raising dinner in a manner that is unambiguous, convincing and courteous.

Finally, request the Official who would receive your correspondence to place it before the President at the earliest opportunity. Remember that you are addressing a top government personage, who may sometimes consider himself or herself even more important than the President. You should therefore avoid words and expressions that might suggest an order or a command. If you don't, you may get into trouble.

1.4   Correspondence to Forward Letters in a Foreign Language

Forwarding letters written in languages other than the *lingua franca* of the addressee creates the greatest difficulty for young officers. But the more experienced officers are usually not exempt from this challenge. The difficulty derives from two principal causes. First, we try to pile up lots of information in one sentence to the extent that the sentence becomes winding, unwieldy and ambiguous. Secondly, we may have become enslaved to habit—the way our predecessors used to do it. And once we've gotten entangled in this mindset, change is hard, and sometimes almost impossible.

Generally, a letter written in a foreign language comes with its *Unofficial Translation.* There are, of course, instances when this is not the case. The Officer is then required to improvise an 'unofficial translation'. How he does it is nobody's business! When you have been 'directed' to forward the letter to its highest destination, you are also expected to transmit not only the text in the original language, but also the unofficial translation. How do you pack all this information in one sentence?

Let's suppose that the Nigerian Ambassador to Senegal has just forwarded a letter from the host President to his counterpart in Nigeria. The text of the correspondence is in French, but the Embassy has provided an Unofficial Translation in English. Your task is to forward both texts—French and English—to the State House. If you think it's easy, I'll tell you something: it is not.

I have had the opportunity to watch young public officers *sweat it out* for days when asked to forward a message to other Ministries or State House. Thank Goodness, they are expected to 'show the draft' for vetting before dispatch!

I must confess that I lack the skill to reconstruct some of the drafts produced by younger public officers to forward correspondence when the *unofficial translation* has been attached to the original text is in a foreign language. The following hypothetical construction can help to illustrate some aspects of the difficulty of writing covering letters to forward correspondence written in foreign languages:

> *I am directed to forward herewith a letter written in French and its unofficial translation in English, which was received from the Nigerian Ambassador to Senegal under cover of his letter reference number NIGEMB/DKR/33/Vol VIII dated 25 May 2003 addressed to His Excellency, Chief Olusegun Obasanjo, President and Commander-in-Chief of the Federal Republic of Nigeria by His Excellency Mr. Abdoulaye Wade, President of the Republic of Senegal for your information and any action you may deem fit.*

Breathtaking, isn't it? Now, let's look at this sentence closely and answer the following questions:

- *What do you think about the length of the sentence?*
- *What is the subject matter of the correspondence from President Wade of Senegal?*
- *The sentence contains a number of irrelevant details. What are they?*
- *What's the opinion of the Ministry on the subject matter of the correspondence?*
- *What action does the Schedule Officer request the receiving authority at the State House to take? Is the desired action precise and clear?*

Try to edit the sentence, with the above outline questions as a guide. Compare your final product with the original text. What differences do you notice?

Here are some helpful hints:

- *Length of Sentence: the sentence is too long. The possibility of losing control of long sentences is an ever-present danger.*
- *Subject matter: The officer failed to highlight the subject matter of the correspondence. It should be stated in the forwarding letter.*
- *Irrelevant details: Lots of them. The reference number of the Ambassador's letter is irrelevant to the message. The use of long titles such as 'Commander-in-Chief of the Federal Republic of Nigeria' is also unnecessary, where it would suffice to say simply 'Mr. President.'*
- *Opinion of the Ministry: The Officer failed to include the views of his organization in relation the subject matter of the correspondence. Foreign Ministries have a sacred duty to guide their Governments with expert opinion—a prerequisite for effective decision-making.*
- *Proposed action: None. The officer failed to state clearly what he expects the Chief of Staff to do. In some ways, he has left the Chief of Staff to 'sort it out himself.' This is a clever way to turn your organization into a General Post Office!*

1.4.1 Simplified Options

Traditionally, we begin correspondence to forward messages with, 'I am directed to...' With this formulation, your sentence gets complicated, especially when, as we've noted in the preceding example, the correspondence you are forwarding is accompanied with its 'Unofficial Translation.' To overcome this difficulty, I suggest that we begin by skipping the, 'I am directed to...' After all, you would be signing the letter on behalf of the Head of your organization any way, which is a clear and adequate proof that you are acting under authority!

So, it is good practice to simplify your sentences by looking for ways to eliminate unnecessary words and phrases that may blur the meaning of your correspondence. Here's a simplified message, forwarding correspondence:

Enclosed please find the original text of a message from His Excellency (name of sender and designation) to His Excellency, (name of addressee and designation). The unofficial translation is attached. The message is in connection with (Subject of the Message).

The Ministry is of the view that (state the opinion of your organization). Accordingly and, having regard to our national interest, we recommend that (state the recommendation).

It will be appreciated if you would arrange to place the said correspondence before His Excellency (name and designation of addressee) at the earliest opportunity.

Sign (name of Official and Designation)
For: (Chief Executive of Organization)

Or the following variant is also acceptable:

Enclosed please find the original text of a message (with its unofficial translation) from His Excellency, Mr. (name of sender and designation) to His Excellency (name of addressee and designation) for transmission to its highest destination.

Thank you for your usual cooperation.
Signed (name of official and designation)
For: (Chief Executive of Organization)

The second formulation should be used with great care. First, it assumes familiarity with the primary receiving authority of the correspondence. It would be impudent to adopt this formulation if that is not the case. Secondly, the subject matter of the correspondence must be such that the opinion of the organization is unnecessary. Otherwise, you would discover it's the quickest way to turn your Ministry or organization into a General Post Office

2

Correspondence with Diplomatic Missions

Written communication between Foreign Ministries and Diplomatic Missions is done in a range of standard formats or formulae. Although variations in detail may occur according to local customs, the modes of correspondence follow a given pattern. It goes without saying that an important deviation from an internationally agreed format of a given type of correspondence would suggest incompetence, amateurism or lousiness on the part of the Ministry's Officials.

Besides, the choice of words and expressions, as well as the type and size of paper to be used is important in this form of correspondence. Words must be chosen with discretion. They must be such as to convey the desired meaning of your message, without hurting the sensibilities of decent men and women. Put differently, the words we use in diplomatic correspondence must not betray a sense of overt hostility or impropriety, regardless of how we may feel.

2.1   The Third Person Note

The *Third Person Note* (also referred to by some writers as 'Official Note in the third person') is the standard form of correspondence between Ministries of Foreign Affairs and Diplomatic Missions It is also the customary mode of communication between Missions.

2.1.1   Common Features of *Third Person Notes*

The *Third Person Note* is typed double-space on the Official Paper (foolscap size) bearing the national crest and address of the Ministry,

Embassy or High Commission. In some countries, *Third Person Notes* may bear only the national crest without the address of the Foreign Ministry or Diplomatic Mission.

Third Person Notes have clearly identifiable parts, including:

(a)   Reference
This is the reference number of the Third Person Note. It is usually inserted on the top right-hand or left-hand corner of the official **paper**.

(b)   Opening:
The *Third Person Note* begins with a formula of courtesy as follows:

> *The Ministry of Foreign Affairs of the Federal Republic of (name of country issuing the Note) presents its compliments to the Embassy/ High Commission of (name of country of the Diplomatic Mission) and has the honour to inform the esteemed Embassy/High Commission that ...*

A variant of this formulation may be:

> *The Ministry of Foreign Affairs of the Federal Republic of (name of State issuing Note) presents its compliments to the Embassy/High Commission of the (name of country of Diplomatic Mission) and has the honour to bring to their attention the following matter...*

This formulation may also be modified as follows:

> *The Ministry of Foreign Affairs of (name of State issuing Note) presents its compliments to the Embassy/High Commission of the (name of country of Diplomatic Mission) and has the honour*

To inform them as follows:
If an Embassy or High Commission issues the Third Person Note, the formulation would be the same. For example, the Opening formula of courtesy would be as follows:

> *The Embassy (or High Commission) of the Republic of (name of country issuing the Note) presents its compliments to the Ministry of Foreign Affairs of the Federal Republic of (name of host country) and has the honour to inform the esteemed Ministry of Foreign Affairs) that....*

Or the formulation of the opening may be varied, depending on the subject of the Note, as in this example:

> *The Embassy (or High Commission) of the Republic of (name of country issuing the Note) presents its compliments to the Ministry of Foreign Affairs of (name of host country) and has the honour to bring to the attention of the esteemed Ministry the following matter:*

(c) Subject-matter of Third Person Notes

This is the body or substance of the Note. Whether you wish to convey the position of your government on a current international issue, or you desire the assistance of the Embassy or High Commission to process visa applications of Members of the National Assembly, the subject-matter of the Note must be expressed in a clear, unambiguous and courteous language.

In *Third Person Notes*, every effort must be made to avoid confusion in the use of personal pronouns. For instance, 1st or 2nd person personal pronoun such as 'I' or 'You' must not be used. If you do, you'd give out yourself as an ignoramus or thoroughly incompetent.

(d) Ending of Third Person Notes:

As with its Opening, *Third Person Notes* end with a formula of courtesy, as in the following example:

> *The Ministry of Foreign Affairs of the Federal Republic of (name of country issuing the Note) avails itself of this opportunity to renew to the Embassy/High Commission of the Federal Republic of (name of country of Diplomatic Mission) the assurances of its highest consideration.*

The ending of Third Person Notes may vary from country to country. For instance, the following formulation is also acceptable:

> *The Embassy (or High Commission) of the Federal Republic of (name of Diplomatic Mission) takes this opportunity of assuring the esteemed Ministry of Foreign Affairs of the Federal Republic of (name of host country) of its highest consideration.*

In some countries, such as the United States, this final courtesy is omitted.

(e) Date, Initials and Official Stamp:

Third Person Notes terminate with the *Date* that the Note was issued. The date is usually typed at the extreme left-hand corner of the official paper, while the *official stamp* of the issuing power is placed at the extreme right-hand corner. The name of the Diplomatic Mission or the Foreign Ministry, whichever is the issuing authority, is inserted below the official stamp and initialed.

(f) Addressee:

Finally, the name and address of the Diplomatic Mission or Foreign Ministry—that is, the intended recipient of the Note—is typed at the bottom left-hand corner of the official paper, below the date. The name and address of the would-be recipient of the Note are reproduced on the envelope.

2.1.2 When to use *Third Person Notes*

The *Third Person Note* offers an unlimited opportunity for communication between Diplomatic Missions and Ministries of Foreign Affairs, as between Diplomatic Missions. It may be used as a vehicle to convey messages, make a complaint, request for an appointment, seek support for the election of your national to an international post, make a proposal or state the position of your government in an ongoing international dispute, etc.

Let's suppose that you are the Chargé d'Affaires *ad interim* of your country's Embassy to Rome. A delegation of your National Assembly is attending a weeklong conference in a remote city of Italy on Child Trafficking. You are planning to host the delegation to a dinner the next day when the conference would end. You receive an urgent call that the local police have arrested a female member of the delegation on charges of child trafficking. The lady had been set up by a criminal gang with the intention to embarrass your government. You intervene, and the police authorities quickly release the distinguished lady, with expressions of 'profound apology'. You decide to protest the police action anyway in very strong terms.

The *Third Person Note* is an excellent mode of correspondence in matters of grave concern. It represents the highest mode of official communication between governments, i.e. between Diplomatic Missions and Foreign Ministries. Put differently, a Third Person Note is not a love letter. The Addressee or recipient of a *Third Person Note* takes its content seriously. For this reason, the Addresser or sender must choose words with great care.

Now, let's try this exercise! Draft a *Third Person Note* to your host Ministry of Foreign Affairs to protest the action of the local police as in the above hypothetical example. Compare your draft with colleagues. But remember: mind your language!

2.2 The *Note Verbale*

There is a general tendency to mistake a Note *Verbale* for the *Third Person Note* (Official Note). There are two reasons for this confusion. First, the *Note Verbale* is written in the third person, just like the *Official Note*. Second, the structure or format of a *Note Verbale* is the same as that of an *Official Note*. But the similarity ends there. The *Note Verbale* differs from the *Third Person Note* in terms of purpose and content.

As the name suggests, the *Note Verbale* is used to clarify or reconfirm points that had been raised in a previous conversation. In other words, a *Note Verbale* implies that a previous meeting had taken place between the relevant parties during which some decision must have been reached or points raised. The *Note Verbale* is then used to reconfirm or clarify those issues that may have come up during the previous conversation or meeting.

Let's consider the following scenarios:

Case I
You are at post. Your head of State is scheduled to pay an Official visit to your country of accreditation. The Head of Mission directs you to arrange a meeting with your country's Desk Officer in the host Ministry of Foreign Affairs or State Department to discuss preparations for the State visit. During the meeting, you discuss a number of issues such as flight details, security, size of delegation, airport reception, local engagements, etc.

You return to your Mission in the evening and, the following morning, you submit a quick report to your Head of Mission about your meeting at the Foreign Office. Your head of Mission is happy with your report. The Desk Officer had given assurances that his government had 'put everything in place' to receive your head of State.

But your head of Mission knows that in diplomacy, verbal assurances are sometimes not enough. So, he further directs, "Look, I don't want these people to mess me up. Please send a suitable *Note* to the Foreign Office to reconfirm the substance of your discussion with the Country Officer!"

Which type of 'Note' would you send to the Foreign Office? A *Note Verbale* or a *Third Person Note?*

Case II

The Chief Justice of your country will soon be leading a delegation of seven other Justices to an International Conference, holding in the United States of America. The Office of the Chief Justice sends the Passports of the Justices to your Ministry, with a request to assist them to obtain the United States visas. Your boss turns to you: "Please forward the passports to the Embassy under cover of a suitable *Note."*

Which type of 'Note' would you consider suitable in this instance? A Note Verbale or an Official Note? Make a draft of the 'Note' and compare it with the 'Note' you have prepared for *Case I.* What do you notice about the two Notes? Explain the difference.

2.3   The *Official Letter*

The *Official Letter* is, in fact, a formal *personal letter.* It is used in a variety of situations between Ambassadors/Heads of Mission and Foreign Ministers as between Ambassadors/Heads of Mission among themselves. The Official Letter is also the mode of correspondence between officials of foreign missions and their counterparts in the host ministries of foreign affairs.

The Official Letter is used most commonly in *semi-official* correspondence. That is not to suggest that the content of such letters is less official than that of the Note Verbale or Third Person Notes. A major difference between Official Letters and *Third Person Notes* is that the former is personalized (i.e. written in the first person) while the latter, as we've seen, is strictly formal and written in the third person. Unlike the *Note Verbale* or the *Third Person Note,* the Official Letter is written on a letter-head or correspondence paper.

Let's suppose your head of Mission desires to make a proposal to the Foreign Minister of your host country or to seek clarification on the position of his government concerning an issue of importance to your country. The draft of your letter should be in the form of an *official letter* written in the first person. You will appear unduly officious if you adopt the format of a *Third Person Note* or a Note Verbale for your draft! The same principle would apply in any correspondence between foreign ministry officials and their colleagues in diplomatic missions and consular posts.

2.3.1 Format of Official *Letter*

Younger officers are frequently required to prepare drafts of correspondence for Ministers and Ambassadors/Heads of Mission when they desire to communicate with each other. Some Ministers and non-career Ambassadors/Heads of Mission believe that the Note *Verbale* is the only form of the correspondence between Foreign Ministries and Diplomatic Missions! This is incorrect. So, when your non-career Ambassador/Head of Mission 'directs' you to, "Please do me a *Note Verbale* to the Ambassador of Tunisia," you should first determine the nature of information he wishes to convey to the embassy. This will help you to advise him on the appropriate form of correspondence—a Note Verbale or Official Letter.

As we have noted, Notes Verbale and Third Person Note are used in strictly official correspondence between governments. Unlike official letters, which are written in the *first person*, Notes Verbale and Third Person Notes are written in the *third person* and they are impersonal. Put differently, the official letter assumes a degree of familiarity—real or imagined—between the parties. The Note Verbale doSo, the Ambassador/Head of Mission who wishes to write to the Foreign Minister of his host country should consider the official letter format. In this case, the letter would begin with either of the following modes of salutation:

- *Your Excellency*
- *Excellency*
- *Sir*

The Salutation, also known as *l'appel*, is usually followed by:
I have the honour to...

The letter may close with either of the following formulations:
I avail myself of this opportunity to assure Your Excellency of my highest consideration.

Or
Please accept, Excellency, the renewed assurances of my highest consideration.

On the other hand, the Ambassador/Head of Mission may vary the salutation and closing of the official letter, depending on his or her relationship with the Foreign Minister. For example, if the Ambassador/Head of Mission is well acquainted with the Foreign Minister, he may use any of the following salutations:

- *My dear Minister of Foreign Affairs,*
- *My dear Secretary of State, etc.*

The closing of the Official Letter would be:

Yours sincerely

Although this form of closing may be typed, it is generally inserted in *long hand* to emphasize the personalized character of the correspondence. Indeed, most experienced Ambassadors/Heads of Mission and Ministers prefer to write, rather than type, the Salutation of Official Letters. If this is the case, the Secretary should leave ample space—four or more single-line spaces—between the *Inside Address* and the Title/Subject-matter of the letter. The writer will insert the appropriate salutation in the space provided for that purpose.

I recall the reaction of the Chief Executive of an Organization when his Bilingual Secretary presented for signature the text of an Official Letter addressed to the Head of a Foreign Mission in his country. The space provided for the Salutation was insufficient. The Chief Executive took a good look at the letter, grimaced and, then sighed, "Oh God, this stupid Secretary hasn't left any space for me to write!" After a while, he managed to squeeze in the *Salutation* and the *Closing* without uttering another word. But the Bilingual Secretary got the message. He knew immediately that, the next time, he might be looking for another job!

Here's a sample Official Letter, showing the spaces for Salutation (*l'appel*) and concluding phrase (also known as *la courtoisie*):

MINISTRY OF FOREIGN AFFAIRS
(OFFICE OF THE MINISTER OF FOREIGN AFFAIRS)

Ref: MDA/SS/SSS/Vol. 24   26 January, 2006

(Space for Salutation in longhand)

Waiver of Visa Interview for Dignitaries
I write to bring to the attention of Your Excellency the concern of my Government over the new visa policy of your Embassy and its potential to undermine the excellent relations which happily exists between our two countries.

The new visa policy requires that all applicants, regardless of their status, will henceforth present themselves   for interview. They would also be required to submit the original copy of their Birth Certificates and First School Leaving Certificates as well as demonstrate, to the satisfaction of the Consular Officer, that they can sing the National Anthem of your great country.

Your Excellency, I am concerned that the new policy does not appear to have taken full account of the sensitivities of our people in matters of age and social status. The application of this policy to Members of our National Assembly and Royal Fathers will arouse anger and resentment.

Your Excellency is aware that, over the past three decades, the great leaders of our two countries have worked hard to promote friendship and cooperation among our peoples. The rapid growth of our current trade and investment figures owes much to the liberal visa policies of our governments. In 2001 alone, 2 million of our nationals visited the Republic of Canary, while 3 million of your citizens came here for business or leisure. These figures represent an increase of 8 percent over the preceding year. I should add, Excellency, that seventy-five percent of our nationals who visit your great country are dignitaries, including National Assembly members and their Royal Highnesses. In economic terms, these visits resulted in 5 percent growth rate for our two countries. Your Excellency will agree that it is in our mutual interest to sustain these gains rather than destroy them.

I therefore request, in the interest of the excellent relations between our countries, that you take early measures to review the new visa policy as it applies to our Legislators and Royal Fathers.

Please accept, Excellency, the assurances of my highest consideration.

(Space for signature)

(Name of person writing the petition)
Minister of Foreign Affairs

Her Excellency Ms Sandra Tournbul
Ambassador
Embassy of The Republic of Canary
209 Quaker Avenue
Abuja

In the above example, the Minister of Foreign Affairs may choose to begin with, *My dear Ambassador*, and end with *Yours sincerely.* In this case, the 'Closing' formula of courtesy (*Please accept the assurances of my highest consideration*) would be unnecessary.

2.4 Correspondence Between Officials of Diplomatic Missions

As a general rule, the official letter is the common form of communication between Officials of Foreign Ministries and Diplomatic Missions. It is similar to the form of correspondence between Ambassadors/Heads of Missions and Foreign Ministers, except that Officials do not address themselves as 'Excellencies. Indeed, correspondence between Officials begins with, 'My dear (*name of the addressee*)' and ends with, 'yours sincerely (*name of the sender*)'. Officials may use their first or last names, depending on the degree of familiarity between the sender and the addressee.

2.5 When to use Official Letters

The Official Letter may be used for virtually any subject. It may be used to acknowledge the receipt of messages, make a request or complaint, solicit assistance, report an incident, or introduce someone to the mission. It is an effective way to communicate directly with those who have responsibility to deal with the issues at stake.

Suppose your national has been taken hostage by angry youths in a remote region of your host country. The embassy may choose to bring the incident to the attention of the Ministry of Foreign Affairs through a *Note Verbale*. It may also decide to rush a letter to the official directly responsible for such matters in the host Foreign Ministry.

The *Official Letter* has one obvious advantage over the *Note Verbale* as a mode of correspondence between officials of Embassies and Foreign Ministries. Because it is personal, its action is fast. The Embassy or Ministry official who receives an official letter (addressed to him in person) will tend to give it his best attention. Unlike the *Note Verbale*, which is somewhat like an 'orphan', the Official Letter speaks to the addressee in his personal capacity, even though the subject matter is certainly official.

Example

The following is a sample semi-official letter between a Foreign Ministry and an Embassy Official. The letter may or may not have a title. The form of salutation, 'My dear Koffi' (or My dear Dr. Oudrogou) underscores the degree of familiarity between the parties. As much as possible, the sender should *write,* and not type, the Salutation and the Closing, Writing the *Salutation* and the *Closing* phrases in the sender's own handwriting enhances the personalized nature of the correspondence:

MINISTRY OF FOREIGN AFFAIRS
TRADE AND INVESTMENT DIVISION

Ref: MFA/XYZ/Vol.1
26 January 2006

(Space for Salutation in long-hand)

Conference On The Africa Growth and Opportunity Act
I am pleased to inform you that my Department will be hosting an international Conference on the Africa Growth and Opportunity Act (AGOA) from 10 –15 December 2006. I recall that your Mission sponsored a similar workshop a few months ago and I was delighted to note that you've acquired tremendous expertise on the subject. I am wondering if you would like to attend our conference to share your experience with other participants from over 150 experts from the WTO, ILO and the United States Department of Commerce, who will be attending.

I should appreciate it Koffi, if you would make time to attend the conference from 10-15 December 2006. Please call me anytime on 095553333 or 080441778109 to confirm your participation.

(Closing courtesy and Signature)

(Name and Designation of Officer)
(Trade and Investment Division)

Dr. Koffi Ouadrogou
Minister (Economic Relations)
High Commission of the Republic of Ghana

In the above example, you will notice the informal character of the letter. The tone of the correspondence is relaxed and underscores the degree of familiarity between the parties. Notice also measures taken by the Ministry Official to persuade his colleague at the High Commission to endeavour to attend the conference.

3

Advanced Correspondence

3.1 Correspondence between Heads of State

Heads of State often communicate with one another through Foreign Ministers, Special Envoys, Ambassadors/Heads of Mission or some other distinguished nominees. However, there are occasions when the need arises for Heads of State to dispatch personal letters to their counterparts in other lands for a variety of reasons. At such times, the letters are written on a special paper bearing the national crest of the sender. They are addressed to the receiver by name, signed and sometimes adorned with the presidential seal of the sender. It would seem that the poorer the country, the more decorated and elegant the special paper!

Indeed, a Head of State may choose to write personally to his or her colleagues for several reasons. There might be need to invite them to special events, to express condolences, or to submit proposals on issues of mutual interest. A Head of State may solicit the support of his counterparts for the candidature of his nationals for vacant posts in International Organizations. Or he might wish to call an Extra-ordinary Summit, as in the case of regional bodies when the eruption of a crisis in a member-State would make it desirable to convene a summit of Heads of State at a short notice.

Besides, special occasions and events entail enormous responsibility at the highest level of government and, in such instances, Heads of State are expected to communicate directly with their colleagues *in writing*. For example, the appointment and recall of ambassadors, dispatch of Special Envoys, Conferment of Full *Powers* to negotiate and sign treaties on behalf of governments and the Declaration of War, represent important moments in inter-state relations when Heads of State must personally address specially-worded correspondence to their counterparts in other lands.

Why is this so?

The signature of a Head of State confers authority to a piece of correspondence. It expresses the importance that the sender attaches to the issue under consideration. So, regardless of its format, the correspondence from one Head of State to another demands special care. It must not be treated as a regular correspondence. It calls for extreme care in construction and style. The tone of the correspondence must be 'presidential!' Put differently, correspondence between Heads of State must reflect the dignity of the personalities behind the words.

Of course, Heads of State usually do not write their own letters. Forget about professional praise singers and hired image makers who would tell us that president this and president that write their own letters! That is not to say that some Presidents lack the skill to write successful official letters to their colleagues. The point is that, even if they wanted to, and do have the training and ability to do so, they cannot afford the stressful time that is often required to prepare a respectable official letter.

But, don't be deceived. Most Heads of State are able to recognize well-crafted letters when they see them. So, when you're required to draft an official letter from your Head of State to another, you must sit up, roll your sleeves and work.

3.2 The *Opening* of Presidential Correspondence

The format of presidential correspondence is similar to the standard Official Letter that we've described in the preceding chapter. However, there are differences in the opening lines, especially among leaders of theocratic states as well as between African Heads of State.

Indeed, African Heads of State have developed a convention of some sort in their written correspondence with one another. They usually address themselves as, *Mr. President and Dear Brother'*. This tradition would seem to have originated from the African Diaspora in Europe and North America. For example, an African Head of State who wishes to write his colleague on the Continent would usually begin his letter (i.e. the *Salutation*) with these words:

Mr. President and Dear Brother.
So, it would be unusual for an African Head of State to address the President of the Republic of China as 'Mr. President and dear Brother', no matter the extent of the personal affinity between them! Instead, the African president will do well to use neutral and non-committal formulations such as the following:

- *Mr. President, ...*
- *Mr. President and Dear Friend, ...*

On the contrary, leaders of theocratic States, that is, countries that have adopted an official or State religion, usually begin official correspondence with the invocation of the Deity upon the addressee such as:

May the Blessings of Allah the Great be upon you!

This is followed by either of the following formulations:

Mr. President and Dear Brother, or simply, Mr. President. .

In general, correspondence between Heads of State does not bear titles. In other words, the subject matter of the correspondence is not stated as in a regular Official Correspondence. Instead, the writer launches into the body of the letter immediately after the *salutation.* However, the central idea of the correspondence must be clearly stated in the opening paragraph or immediately after the pleasantries!

3.3   The *Body* of Presidential Correspondence

Besides the Opening of written correspondence between Heads of State, the body of the letter is equally important. Words must be chosen in a manner to avoid ambiguity. There're a number of reasons for this. Whatever gets out of the lips of a Head of State has implications for his country and its relations with other nations. It is policy. So, the choice of words must express exactly the thought and the mood of the sender.

Remember: confusion in meaning arising from lousy sentence patterns or careless choice of words can 'land' your country in trouble.

Some years ago, a former US President rattled the leaders of the former Soviet Union when he said something like, "We gonna start bombing Moscow in ten minutes!" The story was told that the US President was testing a hotline between Washington and Moscow. Unaware that the US President was testing a new telephone line, Soviet leaders took the American seriously and the world got really agitated and nervous! Obviously, the Soviets would have reacted differently if a lesser mortal had uttered the same words.

3.4   Closing of Presidential Correspondence

There's no universally accepted format for the closing of presidential correspondence. It is therefore important that we study the peculiarities of individual countries in this matter. In practice, however, the following formulations are some common ways to close official correspondence between Heads of State:

(i)   *Closing like an Official Letter:*

Please accept, Mr. President and Dear Friend, the assurances of my highest consideration, etc.;

Please accept, Mr. President, the assurances of my highest consideration.

(ii)   *Fraternal Closing:*

Please accept, Mr. President and Dear Brother, my best wishes for your personal well-being and the continued peace, happiness and prosperity of the government and people of (name of the country).

Common Forms of Presidential Correspondence

In the previous section, we noted that Heads of State correspond with one another for a variety of reasons. The following are some of the most common types of communication between Presidents:

- Condolences
- Congratulatory Messages
- Special Invitation
- Appointment of Ambassadors and Consuls General
- Appointment of a Special Envoy
- Proposals on matters of mutual interest, etc.

4.1   Condolence Letters

Tragedies are commonplace in our world. Natural and man-made disasters strike daily in the remotest parts of the world. And, thanks to modern communication technology, tragic occurrences in one part of the world are viewed all over the globe just as they are happening. In such situations, friendly nations, even the not-so-friendly ones, are expected to dispatch messages of sympathy to the grieving nation. Similarly, the death of a prominent figure in one country such as the head of state or some other eminent person calls for a condolence letter from one Head of State to another.

Whatever may be the cause of the disaster, the tone of the condolence message should be such as to convey the gravity and solemnity of the occasion. Most importantly, the expression of sorrow by the sending Head of State must be genuine and proportional to the event. Any discrepancy between the scale of the disaster and the emotion of the writer will naturally betray his insincerity, which can irretrievably damage the essence of the condolence message. Besides, you must get your facts right.

Let's suppose that an earthquake has struck in Iran. Initial estimates indicate that over 20,000 lives have been lost, 30,000 persons are injured and property worth $500 million destroyed. By any standard, this represents a national tragedy, which calls for international action and sympathy.

If you are required to prepare a draft letter of condolence from your President to the President of the Republic of Iran, you will need to obtain answers to the following questions:

- What is the casualty rate of the tragedy?
- What is the cause of the tragedy?
- Where did the tragedy occur, i.e. in which region or province of the country did the earthquake occur?
- What form of assistance does the affected country require?
- Which country or countries have already provided assistance?
- What form of assistance can your country offer in the disaster?

Facts are sacred to persuade your reader to believe you. Put differently, the more facts you can build into your message, the more the likelihood that you will be credible. The reader will tend to believe that you have taken pains to research the tragedy and this will show that you are genuinely interested in the affairs of the grieving country and its people.

4.1.1 The Concept of Time
Time is a critical factor in condolence messages. For this reason, Heads of State compete with one another in the race to become the first to deliver a letter of condolence to the nation in difficulty. The grieving State should receive the condolence message when the tragedy is still fresh in the minds of the people, preferably either on the same day, or a day or two immediately after the disaster. If the letter arrives late— say, a week or two after the tragedy—the addressee may consider the letter as an after-thought.

4.1.2 Transmission of Letters of Condolence

Messages of condolence are rarely signed personally by Heads of State. In practice, Foreign Diplomatic Missions are expected to write and convey Letters of Condolence on behalf of their Heads of State to the host authorities through *Third Person Notes*. The Letters will usually end with the following expression:
"Signed: (the name of the sending Head of State)."

In such cases, Heads of Mission are required to inform their Headquarters (i.e. Ministry of Foreign Affairs) about the action they have taken, along with a copy of the Letter of Condolence. This approach is helpful in the sense that it allows the sending State to communicate its sympathy and support, if any, to the grieving nation almost immediately the tragedy has occurred.

Here's a sample Letter of Condolence written and delivered by a Head of Mission to his host authorities in time of national emergency:

The Embassy of the Federal Republic of (Name of sending State) presents its compliments to the Ministry of Foreign Affairs of the (Name of receiving State) and has the honour to transmit hereunder the text of a Letter of Condolence from His Excellency (Name of Sending Head of State), President of the Republic of (Name of country) to His Excellency, Mr. (Name of host Head of State), President of (Name of receiving State) following the recent earthquake that devastated parts of the Republic of (name of host State):

Message Begins:
"I have received with shock and horror the news about the massive earthquake that struck the South-eastern region of your great country on (date of the event), resulting in the loss of thousands of innocent lives and large-scale destruction of property and essential infrastructure.
"On behalf of the Government and People of the Federal Republic of (Name of Sending State) and on my own behalf, I send to Your Excellency, the Government and People of the Republic of (Name of the receiving State) my heartfelt condolence over this tragedy.
We share your pains at this time of national grief and pray that the Almighty God would grant Your Excellency, the Government and

People of the Republic of (Name of receiving State) the wisdom, courage
and fortitude to cope with the aftermath of this tragic incident.
> *Please accept, Mr. President, the renewed*
> *assurances of my highest esteem.*
> Signed (Full Name of Sending Head of State)

His Excellency, Mr. (Name of Head of State)
President of the Republic of (Name of Country)
Presidential Villa
(Name of Capital City)"

Message Ends

The Embassy of the Federal Republic of (Name of
Country's Diplomatic Mission) avails itself of this
opportunity to renew to the Ministry of Foreign Affairs
of the Republic of (Name of the Receiving State) the
assurances of its highest consideration.

Date, Official Stamp and Initials

Ministry of Foreign Affairs of (Name of Receiving State)
(Full Address of the Ministry).

The above sample Condolence Letter may be adapted to suit
different situations that require expressions of commiseration. For
example, the death of a Head of State or other national leaders and
eminent persons calls for condolence messages, which must be
dispatched in a timely manner. However, the nature of relations
between States and their leaders will, in most cases, determine the
desirability or otherwise of Condolence Messages at the highest level.

4.1.3   Letters of Condolence Signed and Sealed
In exceptional circumstances, correspondence relating to Condolence
messages may be signed and sealed by Heads of State. In such
instances, it underscores the importance that the sending State attaches
to its relationship with the receiving State.

Ideally, Heads of State ought to personally sign important
correspondence. Receiving Heads of State place great value on such
correspondence, coming under the seal and signature of their

colleagues in other countries.   But the critical issue of timing makes it rather impracticable for them to do so.

For example, it takes a great deal of time to get the Heads of State to consider the draft from the Ministry of Foreign Affairs and have it retyped in their own personal correspondence paper. The result is that, in most cases, condolence messages arrive too late to serve the desired purpose. To overcome this difficulty, Foreign Missions usually write and deliver such time-sensitive correspondence on behalf of their Heads of Government, even though the impact of the messages has been somewhat diminished.

As much as possible, condolence messages and other important correspondence from one Head of State to another should be signed and sealed by the sending heads of State. Foreign Missions consider such correspondence and similar forms of friendly communication an important diplomatic achievement. They are usually eager to forward them to their respective Headquarters by the fastest means, where it would be interpreted as a measure of their effectiveness in working to improve relations between the sending and receiving States.

4.1.4   Congratulatory Messages

There are a variety of occasions when States are expected to congratulate one another for specific accomplishments or commemoration of historic events. Political Departments of Ministries of Foreign Affairs send and receive messages of congratulation on a daily basis. Messages of congratulation represent one of the forms of expression of friendly relations between countries. Occasions that demand congratulatory messages may include the following:

- National Day Anniversary
- Successful Completion of General Elections
- Election of a new President or Re-election of the incumbent for another term of office
- Hosting of major international events
- Victory of the National Team in an International Competition
- Commemoration of a National Monument,
- Conferment of Honours such as distinguished titles, etc

Whatever may be the occasion, the principle of drafting letters of· congratulation is the same. Think of those frustrating days when an officer takes a whole working day only to produce a shoddy draft Message of Congratulation. Indeed, young diplomats can spend a whole day drafting what, ordinarily may be considered a simple congratulatory letter. The reason is that they are not sure what a standard congratulatory letter should contain.

Young officers can learn the various techniques of writing congratulatory letters on *the job*. But this usually takes many years of patient frustration before they begin to get it right. So, wouldn't it be better and more satisfying to learn and practise the basic principles of writing congratulatory letters as an important aspect of a diplomat's continuous training program? I think so too.

There are two main advantages of learning the principles of writing messages of congratulation. First, you will save your valuable time. Second, you will be able to submit a respectable draft to your boss. And third, you will be able to distinguish a good draft from a mediocre one. Here are some points to bear in mind when required to put a draft letter of congratulation:

(a) The Occasion
What's the occasion? A thorough knowledge of the event or occasion will help you to focus your draft. If you lack an understanding of the occasion, your draft will most likely be vague and purposeless. The addressee may possibly ask a question like this, "What's this guy trying to say." If you make anyone ask this kind of question about your writing, you'd better go home and have three cups of coffee!

(b) The question of Relevance
What's the significance of the occasion to the addressee? There are several ways to obtain information concerning the relevance of the occasion to the addressee. In most cases, your diplomatic Mission in receiving State would have sent a brief to headquarters, giving the background and antecedent of the event or occasion. You should build this information into your draft. Otherwise, call up your Mission and ask for its input. In most cases, the information may not be classified. So, the Mission can send its response by email or fax. If as it happens at times, that you don't have

a diplomatic Mission in the country of the addressee, but the addressee maintains one in your capital, you can discretely find out from the resident Mission what the occasion being celebrated means to sending State. In the alternative, you can search the information you need Online to help you prepare your draft. Your boss will be surprised how "you managed."

(c) Diplomatic Value of the occasion

What is the diplomatic value of the occasion within the framework of the bilateral   relations between the sending and receiving States? For example, what does your country expect to gain from the event or occasion? Would it contribute to improved bilateral relations between your country and the country hosting the occasion?

As one eminent writer said, an example is not the main thing in convincing people. It is the only thing. Let's now take a few examples to illustrate the elements of standard correspondence relating to congratulatory messages.

(i) On the Occasion of a National Day Anniversary

Mr. President,
On behalf of the Government and People of the Federal Republic of (name of sending country) and on my own behalf, I have the pleasure to send to Your Excellency, the Government and People of (name of receiving country) hearty congratulations on the occasion of the (year of event) Independence Anniversary of your great country.
Exactly 35 years today, the Founding Fathers of the Republic of (name of country) waged a heroic struggle against imperialism and hoisted the flag of one of Africa's most stable and prosperous nations. We warmly commend your visionary leadership and the resourcefulness of your people in the face of daunting challenges of nation building, especially the manner in which you achieved national

*reconciliation after the tragic civil war that threatened the
very existence of your country.*

*Mr. President, as we rejoice with Your Excellency, the
Government and People of the Republic of (name of receiving
country) on this Special Day, we look forward to the
opportunity of working with you to expand and strengthen
the excellent relations, which happily subsist between our
two nations and peoples.*

*Please accept, Mr. President, the renewed assurances of my
highest esteem.*

Name of sending Head of State)
(President, Federal Republic of (name of country)

The above example consists of *four paragraphs*. Each paragraph
represents an important aspect of the Message. The paragraphs are
connected logically to each other, and to the whole Message as well.
For example, the opening paragraph (i.e. paragraph 1) expresses the
felicitation, which is the heart of the message. Paragraph 2 evokes
the justification or rationale for the event. Why is the National Day
worth celebrating? Paragraph 3 touches on the diplomatic implication
of the event—the desire of the sending State to seize the opportunity
(i.e. the National Day) to call for stronger bilateral relations with the
receiving State; and paragraph 4 concludes with a formula of courtesy.

There are times when writers may decide to skip paragraph 2—
i.e. the commendation paragraph. When this happens, it may be that
the Official drafting the message is either lazy or lousy or both.

Whether we believe it or not, flattery is a common feature of the
human condition. We like to be recognized, to be praised and if need
be, to be flattered. But flattery is a tricky business! If you believe that
your message should include a commendation paragraph as in
paragraph 2 above, the schedule officer must find concrete instances
about the leadership of the receiving State to justify the commendation
paragraph. For example, you may need to highlight the major
achievements of past and present leaders of the country. Have they
made a difference in the lives of their people?

In some countries, most citizens are indifferent to the National Day celebration. At best, they see National Day events simply as another opportunity for the leadership to siphon public funds. In such cases, do not   attempt to invent acts of heroism if you have *nothing to declare*. The message will sound false!

Put differently; do not force yourself to praise the leadership of the receiving state, if you have no reasons to do so. Remember the adage: honesty is the best policy.   If we try to praise the leadership when you truly believe there are   no reasons to do so, the audience will see through the gaping hole in your congratulatory letter and its credibility would be impaired.

(ii) On The Election As President or Head of State

The format of correspondence to send messages of congratulation on the occasion of election as president is similar to that of the National Day that we've just described. For example, the writer begins by first congratulating the victorious president on his election. He then goes on to state the possible reasons that may have persuaded the electorate. The use of such trite expressions as 'your sterling qualities' and 'your indefatigable leadership spirit,' etc, should be avoided. They are vague and may even smack of hypocrisy. It is possible the new president may have won the election by means other than fair. So, if you waste your time complimenting him, he surely will not believe you. Deep in his heart, he would think you're either dishonest or merely wish to make a mockery of him.

To be credible therefore, a good congratulatory message   should contain   specific instances of heroism or contribution to the public good. Generalities and platitudes are of no help. In the case of election or re-election to the high office of president, the individual may have won the hearts of the electorate with policies and programs, which they believe, would improve their lives and circumstances.   So, in drafting messages of congratulation, we should identify those policies that may have contributed to the candidate's electoral victory.

Two things are possible when we have difficulty finding specific or probable reasons for an electoral victory. Either we've failed to do a thorough research on the conduct of the elections, or there may be no tangible reasons to justify the landslide victory after all. In such cases, don't 'go to town' to invent reasons to justify the candidate's electoral success, as this might plunge you into platitudes and banalities.

As one writer said, " it takes a wise a man to tell a lie. A fool had better say the truth!"

So, when in doubt, most cautious writers would prefer to skip the commendation paragraph and move on to the next, as in the following example:

Mr. President and Dear Brother,

On behalf of the Government and People of the Federal Republic of (Name of country of addresser) and on my own behalf, I congratulate you for your election as President of the Republic of (Name of the country of addressee).

I take this opportunity to reaffirm the desire of my Government and people of (Name of country of sender) to work with your new Administration to further strengthen the bonds of friendship, understanding and mutual respect that have, over the years, characterized the relations between our two countries.

Please accept, Mr. President and Dear Brother, the assurances of my highest esteem.

(Name of host president)

President of the Federal Republic of (Name of country)

4.1.5   Correspondence relating to Letters of Invitation

There are occasions when a president may desire to invite his colleagues to events of national or international significance. Such events might include the inauguration of the National Assembly, commemoration of a National Monument, commissioning of an Industrial facility, Anniversary of the National Day, and the Opening Ceremony of an International Conference, among other such occasions.

Also, your government may find it desirable to invite a foreign Head of State to a national event as Special Guest, Guest of Honour or Guest Speaker. For example, the host president may consider that the Opening Session of the National War College Course for Senior Military Officers will present an opportunity to make an important policy statement on military-government relations in Africa. He may decide to add an international perspective to the event by inviting a distinguished foreign Head of State whose knowledge and experience would help to enrich the content of the occasion.

In principle, a letter of invitation, like all presidential correspondence, must be written in ornate style and with great care.

And as much as possible, the letter should contain some or all of the following points:

- Purpose of the invitation;
- Significance of the occasion to the country;
- Role that the Special Guest would be expected to play, if any;
- Who else would be invited (especially in the case of Presidents);
- Antecedent of the event, if any. Is this the first time you are hosting it?
- Date, time and venue of the event;
- Hospitality and protocol. For example,: who would pay the   bill and who would receive the Special Guest? Etc
- Any other relevant information to persuade the Special Guest to honour the invitation.   For example, why do you think he should attend the event and, how would his inability to come hurt your relations, etc?

Consider the following example:

> Mr. President and Dear Brother,
> *In furtherance of the excellent relations between our two countries, I have the pleasure to invite you as Special Guest of Honour to an International Conference on Conflict Resolution, holding in (venue of the conference) on 30 June 2005. The theme of the Conference is Managing African Conflicts For Development In the 21st Century.*
> *Mr. President, you will recall that since the early 1980's, virtually every African country has experienced one form of conflict or the other. Out of the 53 independent African States, 30 have fought wars with their neighbours. This figure represents over 70 percent of the countries on the Continent, which have either fought wars already or, given current indicators, would fight in the very near future. Besides, 10 other African nations are engaged, to varying degrees, in deadly conflicts within their borders.*
> *What is more disquieting, Mr. President, is the rapid spread of civil conflicts to those countries that, in the last 10 years, were regarded as oasis of peace and stability in our conflict-ridden Continent. (Give some examples). The implication of this development is obvious: No single African nation can reasonably consider itself immune from the virus of conflicts within or outside its borders. If it doesn't happen*

today, it may be tomorrow. Regrettably, the success of modern conflict resolution approaches has been marginal.

The cost of African conflicts in human and material terms has been enormous. Ninety-six percent of the world's Least Developed Countries are in Africa. As leaders, I believe we have an obligation— and an urgent one too—not only to our individual States but also to Africa and the international community to confront the scourge of conflicts without further delay. To this end, my country will host an International Conference on Conflict Resolution on 30 June 2006 at (venue). Participants will be drawn from a wide range of expert sources including the United Nations, the Universities, Organizations of Labour, the Civil Society and International Federation of Presidential Aspirants.

Presidents (name of presidents/countries) and the Secretary General of the United Nations have assured me that they would be present at the Opening Ceremony.

I am aware, Mr. President, of your expertise on this subject, having successfully mediated the longest and the most brutal conflict in your sub-region. The Conference will undoubtedly present an opportunity to share your experience with the many distinguished participants. I will therefore appreciate it if you would arrange to confirm your participation, especially your availability to deliver the Keynote Address at the Opening Session on 30 June 2006.

Please accept, Mr. President and dear Brother, the assurances of my highest consideration.

(Name of host president)
President of (Name of country)

5

Specialized Presidential Correspondence I

5.1 Correspondence Relating to *Letters of Credence*

The appointment of ambassadors represents, at least in principle, the highest expression of friendship between States. There are occasions however, when heads of State may appoint ambassadors to a hostile country when the sending State believes that it is in its national interest to do so. When a Head of State appoints an ambassador to another country, the individual is provided with a *Letter of Credence*, which is proof of his authenticity to the Head of State to which he is accredited. *Letters of Credence* are also referred to as *Credentials*.

Letters of Credence are written in a form and style that might appear superfluous to the uninitiated. But the beauty of diplomatic communication is this passion for color and style. Those who ignore this tradition are either ignorant of the culture of diplomatic correspondence or simply amateurs. A typical *Letter of Credence* would look like this:

> *To (full name and title of the receiving Head of State)*
> *Excellency*
> *I have appointed (name and title of the nominee), a distinguished citizen of (name of the sending State), to represent me before your Government as Ambassador Extraordinary and Plenipotentiary of (name of the sending State).*
> *He is well aware of the mutual interests of our two countries and shares my sincere desire to preserve and enhance the long friendship between us.*

My faith in his high character and ability gives me entire confidence that he will carry out his duties in a manner fully ascertainable to you.
Accordingly, I entrust him to your confidence and I ask that you receive him favorably, and give full credence to what he shall say on the part of (name of the sending State) as well as to the assurances which he bears of my best wishes for the prosperity of (name of the receiving State)

Yours very truly

(Name and Signature of Head of State)

In some countries, a *Letter of Credence* may be more complex than the simple format shown above. In such cases, the following formulation is acceptable:

(Name and title of Sending Head of State)
To
(Name and title of Receiving Head of State)

Being desirous of making provision for the representation in the (Name of the receiving State) of the interests of (Name of sending State) and for the maintenance of relations of amity and concord which so happily exist between the (Name of sending State) and (Name of receiving State), I have chosen (Name and title of the Ambassador-designate) to reside with you in the capacity of Ambassador Extraordinary and Plenipotentiary of the (Name of Sending State).

(Name and title of the Ambassador)'s

Personal qualities and the experience which I have had of his talents and zeal for the service of the government of (Name of the sending State) assure me that his selection will be perfectly acceptable to you, and that he will discharge his duties in such a manner as to merit your approbation and esteem and to prove Himself worthy of this new mark of confidence.
I therefore request that you give entire credence to all that **(Name and title of the Ambassador-designate)** *shall communicate to you in my name, especially when he shall convey to Your Excellency the assurances of the lively interest which my Government takes in*

everything that affects the welfare and prosperity of (Name of the receiving State)

Given at (Name of Capital City of Sending State), this ......Day of...... (Month)......(Year)

(Name, Seal and Signature of sending Head of State)

5.2   Letter of Commission

The Letter of Appointment of an Ambassador is known as a *Commission.* It is not a *Letter of Credence* –the special correspondence from one head of State to another concerning the appointment of a new ambassador. On the contrary, the Ambassador's Commission is a declaration that he has been appointed the Principal Representative of one state in another state for the purpose of advancing the mutual interests of both countries.   Unlike the *Letter of Credence,* the Commission is not addressed to anyone in particular as you can see from the following format:

(NAME OF HEAD OF STATE ISSUING THE COMMISSION)

To All and Singular to whom these Presents shall come, Greetings!
Whereas it appears to me expedient to nominate some Persons of approved Wisdom, Loyalty, Diligence and Circumspection to represent me in the character of Ambassador Extraordinary and Plenipotentiary in (Name of receiving State) with the special object of representing the interest of the Federal Republic of (Name of the country)

Now Know Ye that I, reposing special trust and confidence in the discretion and faithfulness of my Trusty and well-beloved (Name of the ambassador-designate) have nominated, constituted and appointed as I do by these Presents nominate, constitute and appoint him, the said (Name of the ambassador-designate) to be my Ambassador Extraordinary and Plenipotentiary in (Name of receiving State) for the purpose aforesaid.

Giving and Granting to him in that character all Power and Authority to do and perform all proper acts, matters and things which may be desirable or necessary for the promotion of relations of friendship, good understanding and harmonious intercourse between the (Name of the Sending State) and (Name of receiving State) and for the protection and furtherance of the interests confided to his care by the diligent and discreet accomplishment of which acts, matters and things aforementioned he shall gain my approval and show himself worthy of my high confidence.

And I, therefore request all those whom it may concern to receive and acknowledge (Name of the ambassador-designate) as Ambassador Extraordinary and Plenipotentiary as aforesaid and freely to communicate with him upon all matters which may appertain to the objects of the high Mission whereto he is hereby appointed.

Given at (capital city of issuing authority) under my Hand and Seal this. Day of ...... (Month)...... (Year)

(NAME, SIGNATURE OF HEAD OF STATE ISSUING)
(COMMISSION)

5.3   Letter of Appointment of High Commissioners

The letter appointing High Commissioners to Commonwealth countries is similar to that of Ambassador to non-Commonwealth countries. The only difference is in the designation. For example, in place of Ambassador, the appointee will be designated as High Commissioner, as in the following example:

[NAME OF PRESIDENT OF SENDING STATE]
To All and Singular to whom these Presents shall come, Greetings!
Whereas *it appears to me expedient to nominate some Persons of approved Wisdom, Loyalty, Diligence and Circumspection to represent me in the character of High Commissioner in (Name of receiving State) with the special object of representing the interests of the Federal Republic of (Name of the country)*

Now Know Ye *that I, reposing special trust and confidence in the discretion and faithfulness of my Trusty and well-beloved (Name of the High Commissioner-designate) have nominated, constituted and appointed as I do by these Presents nominate, constitute and appoint him, the said (Name of the High Commissioner-designate) to be my High Commissioner in (Name of receiving State) for the purpose aforesaid. Giving and Granting to him in that character all Power and Authority to do and perform all proper acts, matters and things which may be desirable or necessary for the promotion of relations of friendship, good understanding and harmonious intercourse between the (Name of the Sending State) and (Name of receiving State) and for the protection and furtherance of the interests confided to his care by the diligent and discreet accomplishment of which acts, matters and things aforementioned he shall gain my approval and show himself worthy of my high confidence.*

And I, therefore request all those whom it may concern to receive and acknowledge (Name of the High Commissioner-designate) as High Commissioner as aforesaid and freely to communicate with him upon all matters which may appertain to the objects of the high Mission whereto he is hereby appointed.

Given at (capital city of issuing authority) under my Hand and Seal this .... Day of .... (Month) .... (Year)

[NAME OF PRESIDENT OF SENDING STATE]

5.4 Letter of Recall of Ambassadors

When an ambassador has completed his *tour of duty* in the receiving State, he does not just pack his personal effects and leave the country where he had served for three to four years as the case may be. He will be asked to return home by the Head of State who sent him. The letter informing the receiving Head of State of the recall is called *Letter of Recall.*

Once the ambassador has been given notice of the date of his recall, he will be allowed ample time to wind up his affairs during which he is expected to formally take leave of the host Head of State. In some countries, the outgoing ambassador will, during this period, submit his *Letter of Recall* to the host Head of State or President. In other traditions, the ambassador's *Letter of Recall* will be delivered to the host Head of State/President by his successor along with Letter *of Credence* or *Credentials*.

The following is the usual format of a Letter of Recall:

(Name of President of RETURNING AMBASSADOR)
To
(NAME OF President of the HOST STATE)
Having occasion elsewhere for the services of my Trusty and well beloved **(Name of ambassador being recalled)** *who has for sometime been the accredited Ambassador Extraordinary and Plenipotentiary of (Name of sending State) in the (Name of receiving State), I have thought it fit to notify you of his Recall.*

Having myself had ample reason to be satisfied with the zeal and fidelity with which **(Name of ambassador being recalled)** *executed my orders on all occasions during his Mission, I trust that Your Excellency will also have found his conduct deserving of your approbation and esteem, and in this pleasing confidence, I avail myself of the present opportunity to renew to Your Excellency the assurances of the invariable friendship and my earnest wishes for the welfare and prosperity of the (Name of the receiving State).*

Given at ...(capital city), this ...Day of ...(Month), Two thousand and ...

(Name, Seal and Signature of **President of Returning Ambasador**)

(Name and Address of host)
(Head of State)

6

Specialized Presidential Correspondence II

6. 1   Letter to Introduce a Special Envoy

There are numerous occasions when Heads of State would consider it desirable to send Special Envoys to their counterparts. Usually, such occasions entail matters of some urgency, although in some parts of the world, the dispatch of special envoys is sometimes abused. In practice, special envoys are used when issues of extreme importance and urgency are involved.

Correspondence relating to Special Envoys may vary from country to country. But it has four distinguishing characteristics, namely:

*   Stylized Opening and Closing
*   Profile of the Special Envoy
*   Purpose or Subject of the Special Mission
*   Powers of the Special Envoy

An essential feature of a *Special Envoy* is that he is sent out to accomplish a specific task. The task must be urgent to justify the mission.

Let's look at this scenario:

Country A is landlocked and poor; its economy is totally dependent on money transfers from its nationals resident in its richer and more powerful neighbours, country B. Hungry troops of country A invade a border town of country B without provocation. The President of country A is concerned that the President of country B may retaliate. His worst fear is the possible expulsion of thousands of his nationals from country B. He weighs the social and economic implications of this outcome for his political survival: mass unemployment; resurgence of petty crimes; social discontent and unrest. It's like cutting his nation's economic lifeline right from the middle! The matter is serious enough to deserve immediate response.

So, to underscore the importance and urgency of the situation, the President of country A decides to dispatch a Special Envoy. He must act quickly to reassure the President of country B that the soldiers had acted on their own.

The Letter introducing the Special Envoy may take this form:

Mr. President,

Within the framework of the excellent relations of friendship, solidarity and cooperation which happily exist between our two peoples and nations, I have the great pleasure to introduce to Your Excellency my distinguished, and trusted Special Envoy in the person of (Name and Official Designation of the Envoy).

He is leading a high-powered delegation to Your Excellency in connection with the unfortunate action of some unruly soldiers, which occurred in your border town of ... on 17 February 2004.

I have instructed him to deliver to Your Excellency the present written correspondence and to reassure you of my determination to take prompt and adequate measures, so that this unfortunate incident will never happen again.

It is my fervent hope that, as in the past, our citizens in your territory will continue to enjoy the hospitality, protection and friendship of the brotherly and peace-loving people of (name of country B)

The Special Envoy has my full confidence. I therefore implore Your Excellency to give credence to all that he will say to you on my behalf, especially my renewed sentiments of friendship and high esteem.

Kindly accept, Mr. President, the assurances of my highest consideration.
(NAME AND SIGNATURE OF PRESIDENT)
OF COUNTRY A)

(NAME AND ADDRESS OF PRESIDENT)
(OF COUNTRY B)

6. 2 Head of Official Delegation as Special Envoy

Besides the scenario described above, there are other situations when a Minister or some other Official of Government would lead a national delegation to an international conference. In such instances, the President of the country sending the delegation to the conference may designate the leader of the delegation as his Special Envoy. He would then seize the opportunity to exchange views on issues of mutual interest with the President of the State hosting the conference

Or, the President sending the delegation may simply wish to inform his counterpart of the presence of his Minister or other important persons in his Administration in the other's territory. Again, as in the previous example, the sending President will seize the opportunity to pay his compliments to the receiving Head of State. This gesture is valued as a mark of respect and friendship for the receiving President. It is a courteous act that most experienced Heads of State hardly fail to exploit for political advantage.

6. 3 Special Envoys in Preventive Diplomacy

Similarly, it may be desirable to dispatch a Special Envoy to another Head of State when a sudden change of national policy in one country has occurred, especially when the change may have an impact on the primary interest of other States. For example, a change of immigration policy in one country may be such as to create difficulties for citizens of other countries resident in the country initiating the policy. If the implementation of the new policy leads to the mass deportation or incarceration of citizens of other States, the Head of State initiating the policy may decide to send Special Envoys to the vulnerable States in order to explain the circumstances leading to the change of policy.

This is a desirable proactive step. If he fails to do so, those States whose nationals are likely to suffer under the new policy may misunderstand the intention of the policy. In such situations, the Special Envoy has an important troubleshooting role to play to bridge the communication gap that would otherwise arise between governments.

The following is a sample Letter to Introduce a Special Envoy to a foreign head of State when a change of immigration policy has occurred in one country:

Mr. President and Dear Brother,
In furtherance of the excellent relations that happily exist between our two countries, I have the pleasure to introduce to Your Excellency my worthy and trusted Minister of Foreign Affairs (name and title of the Minister).

As Your Excellency would recall, our security forces foiled an attempt to overthrow my government by force on 16 February 2005. Fifth-five persons—mostly illegal aliens—have been arrested. I regret to say that, of this number, forty-five claim to be nationals of your country.

Mr. President, as a small Island nation, our economy is totally dependent on tourism. Your Excellency will agree, that Tourism cannot thrive in an atmosphere of fear or threats to the peace. The action of the coup plotters was therefore an attack at the very heart of our economy. As a responsible government, we have a duty to take appropriate measures to restore the confidence of the international tourists in our country. To this end, I have ordered an immediate review of our immigration laws to ensure that henceforth, foreigners coming into the Republic must meet stringent criteria. In particular, all aliens wishing to come here must swear to an affidavit that, as long as they reside within our borders, they will not wear long beard.

Mr. President, I have not doubt that, as the most respected and loyal supporter of our country's democracy, you would share our concern in this matter, especially the involvement of your citizens in this unfriendly act. I have therefore instructed my Minister of Foreign Affairs to apprise you of our new immigration policy about which we count on your usual understanding.

Finally, Mr. President, I wish to assure you that my Minister of Foreign Affairs has my confidence. I implore you to give credence to all that he will have occasion to say to you on my behalf, especially when he will express my best wishes for your continued good health, happiness and prosperity.

Please accept, Mr. President and dear brother, the renewed assurances of my highest consideration.

NAME AND SIGNATURE OF THE PRESIDENT

FULL NAME, **DESIGNATION & ADDRESS**
OF THE RECIPIENT HEAD OF STATE

6. 4   Special Envoys in a Pre-Summit Diplomacy

Finally, Special Envoys may serve as an important tool to assess the chances of support for a controversial policy. Let's suppose, for example, that your Head of State has a brilliant idea: Abolish all sovereign African States and establish one Continental Government under a single Military Command! He intends to introduce the proposal at the next summit of the African Union. He is convinced that this proposal would bring an end to the many conflicts in Africa.

Although he believes strongly in the merit of his proposal, he does not expect a standing ovation at the summit! There will be equally strong opposition to this brilliant idea. Most of his colleagues would not be prepared to give up all or part of their sovereignty for the larger interest of Africa! At least, not yet!

So, at this juncture, the Special Envoy becomes a handy tool. His Special Mission is to try to convince most of the Heads of State participating at the summit to give the proposal a chance. He will measure their mood and, if possible, try to persuade them to give the proposal a courteous reception of some sort. The outcome of the Special Mission—a form of pre-summit consultation—will   help to determine the fate of the proposal!

7

Specialized Ministerial Correspondence

There are some classes of correspondence reserved for Ministers of Foreign Affairs. These correspondences are, by diplomatic tradition, signed by Foreign Ministers. They include Letters of Appointment of Charge d'Affaires *en titre*, Letters of Introduction of Acting High Commissioners *en titre*, Letters of Appointment of Consul General, and Full Ppwers, among others.

7. 1 Letter of Appointment of Charge d'Affaires *en titre*

There are two classes of Charge d'Affaires. The first is the *Chargé d'Affaires en titre* and the other, the Chargé d'Affaires *ad interim* or a.i. In some Commonwealth countries, a distinction is also made between the Acting High Commissioner *en titre* and the Acting High Commission *ad interim*.

A Chargé d'Affaires *ad interim* is a Foreign Service Officer who takes charge of a diplomatic Mission temporarily during the absence of an ambassador or substantive Head of Mission. He assumes this important function on the basis of his being the most senior career foreign officer in the Mission at the time. He will automatically cease to function in that capacity as soon as the ambassador or substantive Head of Mission returns to post or one has been appointed.

On the other hand, a Chargé d'Affaires *en titre* or Acting High Commissioner *en titre* is a substantive Head of Mission in the same way as the ambassador. Although the Chargé d'Affaires *en titre* enjoys virtually the same rights and privileges accorded to an Ambassador, he ranks immediately below the ambassador in the *Order of Precedence*.

Accordingly, the Letter appointing the Chargé d'Affaires *en titre* is addressed by the Minister of Foreign Affairs of the sending State to the Minister of Foreign Affairs of the receiving State. This implies that on his arrival at post, the Chargé d'Affaires *en titre* will present his *Letter of Credence* to the Minister of Foreign Affairs of the receiving State and not to the President or Head of State of the receiving State as would an Ambassador.

Here is the format of a *Letter of Credence* of a Chargé d'Affaires *en titre*:

> *(NAME OF FOREIGN MINISTER OF SENDING STATE)*
> *(TO: NAME OF FOREIGN MINISTER OF RECEIVING STATE)*
> *Being desirous of making provision for the representation in the (Name of the receiving State) of the interests of (Name of sending State) and for the maintenance of relations of amity and concord which so happily exist between the (Name of sending State) and (Name of receiving State), I have chosen (Name of the Charge d'Affaires-designate) to reside with you in the capacity of Charge d'Affaires en titre of the (Name of Sending State).*
>
> *(Name and title of the Charge d'Affaires)'s*
> *Personal qualities and the experience which I have had of his talents and zeal for the service of the government of (Name of the sending State) assure me that his selection will be perfectly acceptable to you, and that he will discharge his duties in such a manner as to merit your approbation and esteem and to prove Himself worthy of this new mark of confidence.*
>
> *I therefore request that you give entire credence to all that (Name and title of the Charge d'Affaires-designate) shall communicate to you in my name, especially when he shall convey to Your Excellency the assurances of the lively interest which the Government of (Name of sending State) takes in everything that affects the welfare and prosperity of (Name of the receiving State)*
>
> *Given at (Name of Capital City of Sending State), this ...... Day of: ... ...(Month) ...(Year)*
>
> *NAME AND TITLE AND SIGNATURE AND SEAL*
> *MINISTER OF FOREIGN OF SENDING STATE*

NAME AND TITLE AND ADDRESS
OF MINISTER OF FOREIGN AFFAIRS
OF THE RECEIVING STATE

7. 2 Letter of Introduction of Acting High Commissioner *en titre*

As we noted previously, Letters *of Credence* of Ambassadors are similar to the Letters of Appointment of High Commissioners, except that the latter is known as a *Letter of Introduction*. The principle behind this practice seems to be that the Commonwealth is regarded as a family of nations sharing common historical bonds and peculiarities.

The same is true of the *Letter of Credence* of a Chargé d'Affaires *en titre* and the *Letter of Introduction* of an Acting High Commissioner *en titre* who has been appointed as a substantive Head of Mission. However, some countries take liberty with respect to the format of Letters *of Credence* of Charges d'Affaires *en titre* and Letters of Introduction of Acting High Commissioners *en titre*. In either case, the letter is addressed by the Minister of Foreign Affairs of the sending State to his counterpart in the receiving State.

Example:

> (NAME AND TITLE OF FOREIGN MINISTER OF RECEIVING STATE)
> *Your Excellency,*
>
> *This letter will be presented to you by (Name of the Acting HIGH COMMISSIONER en titre - DESIGNATE), who has been nominated by the Government of (name of sending State) to serve as Ag. High Commissioner en titre of the Republic of (Name of sending State) to the Repubic of (name of receiving State).*
> *I have the honour to request that (NAME OF ACTING HIGH COMMISSIONER EN TITRE- DESIGNATE) be granted such facilities as may be necessary for the effective performance of his functions.*
> *I avail myself of this opportunity to renew to you, the assurance of my highest consideration.*
>
> *Given at ...(capital city of sending State) this ...Day of ....Two Thousand and Six.*
>
> > NAME AND SIGNATURE
> > OF FOREIGN MINISTER OF SENDING STATE.
>
> NAME AND ADDRESS
> OF FOREIGN MINISTER OF RECEIVING STATE

7. 3 Letter of Appointment of Consuls General

There is a great deal of confusion in the use of the terms 'Consul', 'Consular' and 'Consul General'. For instance, it is not uncommon for an enquirer to seek to speak to the 'Consular General' or 'Consulate General' when, in fact, he or she means to speak to the *Consul General*.

A *Consulate* is that branch of the Foreign Service that deals with economic and commercial matters as well as the welfare of nationals of the sending State in the receiving State. I should add quickly that this later function has been largely circumscribed in recent times due to poor funding of most Foreign Services.

Indeed, Consulates perform a wide range of functions. They are concerned with the economic and commercial relations between nations. Originally, diplomatic and consular chores were kept strictly separate because early theorists felt that national interests should not be "tainted" by private commercial matters. Thus, two separate services—diplomatic and consular—usually existed. Today, all major countries have combined these two services, and a single corps of professional civil servants serves in both areas.

Consular work involves a variety of activities. Consuls issue birth, death, and marriage certificates to their citizens residing or traveling in the receiving State. Consular officers also regulate shipping, aid their country's citizens when they travel on business or as tourists, and report on economic and business conditions abroad. Activities are often carried out in consulates located in major trading and commercial cities as well as in the capital city.

The head of a *Consulate General* is known as Consul *General* or 'CG' for short. All other officers of the Consular Post bear the title of *Consul*.

And in view of the variety of functions performed by Consulates *General*, Consuls are identified by the specific functions they perform. For example, you would have *Consul (Commerce);* Consul *(Trade and Investment)*; Consul (Information), etc.

The letter appointing a Consul General is known as *Commission*. It states clearly the duties and obligations of the officer in his or her country of accreditation, as well as the Consular *district(s)* in which he is expected to exercise his function. The following is an example of the *Commission* of a Consul General:

(NAME OF FOREIGN MINISTER OF SENDING STATE)

To All and Singular to who these presents shall come, Greetings!
Whereas the Government of *(name of appointing/sending country)*
is satisfied that it is expedient to appoint a person to exercise the
function of Consul-General in *(name of consular districts and receiving
State)*

And whereas *special trust and confidence are reposed in the
probity, loyalty and zeal of (name of the Consul-General designate)
who has been chosen to assume and exercise the functions aforesaid;*

Now therefore, *on the authority and on the advice of the
Government of (name of sending state), I do constitute and appoint by
these presents the said (name of the Consul-General designate) to be
Consul General of the (name of sending State in (name of consular
districts) conferring upon him all such powers as are appropriate to
his office and requesting for him the recognition, right, privileges
and immunities appertaining thereto.*

*Given at (capital city of sending State), under my Hand and Seal
this.... day of... Two Thousand and ...*
[NAME OF FOREIGN MINISTER OF SENDING STATE]

7. 4   Full Powers

Full Powers represent formal authority given to a delegate to a
conference to participate, negotiate and sign documents that may come
up in the course of the Conference on behalf of his Government.   At
multilateral Conferences where *full powers* are required, a delegate
will not be able to participate unless he has in his possession his full
powers signed by his Foreign Minister.

The following is the format of *Full Power* issued to a delegate
attending a plenipotentiary Conference, i.e. a Conference where
delegates would be required to posses the authority to commit their
governments:

*Whereas, for the better treating of and arranging certain matters
which may come into discussion between the Government of ... and
the Governments of certain other Powers and States represented at the
forthcoming Conference [name of Conference] to be held at ... on, [...]
it is expedient that a fit person should be invested with Full Power to
conduct the said discussion on the part of the Government of; I, [name
in full of Minister for Foreign Affairs], do hereby certify that [...]*

[Name and designation of the leader of the delegation]

is by these Presents named, constituted and appointed as Plenipotentiary and Representative have Full Power and Authority to agree and conclude with such Plenipotentiaries and Representatives as may be vested with similar Power and Authority on the part of the Governments aforesaid any Treaty, Convention, Agreement, Protocol or other Instrument that may tend to the attainment of the above-mentioned end, and to sign for the Government of . . . everything so agreed upon and concluded.

Further, *I do hereby certify that whatever things shall be so transacted and concluded by the said Plenipotentiary and Representative shall, subject if necessary to Ratification by the Government of . . . be agreed to, acknowledged and accepted by the said Government of . .. in the fullest manner.*

In Witness whereof, *I have signed these Presents and affixed hereto my Seal.*

Signed and sealed *at the Ministry of Foreign Affairs (place). The . .. day of. . Two thousand and . . .*

[NAME AND SIGNATURE]
[OF MINISTER FOR FOREIGN AFFAIRS]

7. 5 Governmental Full Power

Governmental Full Power is similar to the *Full Power* given to a Plenipotentiary to sign a Treaty on behalf of his government at a *multilateral Conference*. However, it is used primarily in *bilateral agreements*, where a party to an Agreement demands that the other side designate a person with Full Power to sign the said Agreement on its behalf.

Suppose that officials of the Embassy of the United States and Ministry of Foreign Affairs of Nigeria held a meeting on 19 December 2005. At that meeting, the US Ambassador pledged that his Government would assist Nigeria to construct an ultra modern nuclear facility. The project would take off only after a formal Agreement has been signed between the two countries. To this end, the Government of Nigeria is required to designate a person with *Full*

Power to sign the agreement on its behalf. To give effect to this Agreement, the Governmental Full Power would be like this:

(*NAME OF MINISTER OF FOREIGN AFFAIRS*)

Whereas *at the meeting held in Abuja on 10 December 2005 between Officials of the Embassy of the United States and the Ministry of Foreign Affairs, both sides agreed that the Government of the United States would construct a nuclear facility for Nigeria;*

And Whereas *it was further agreed that the project would take effect after a formal Agreement has been signed between Nigeria and the United States;*

And Whereas *Nigeria is required to designate a person with full power to sign the Agreement aforesaid on its behalf;*

I [name and designation], Minister of Foreign Affairs of the Federal Republic of Nigeria, do hereby certify that

[Name and designation of the person signing the Agreement]
Is by these Presents named, constituted and appointment as Plenipotentiary with full power and authority to sign the aforesaid Agreement in respect of the construction of nuclear facility for Nigeria by the Government of the United States.

In Witness whereof, *I have signed these Presents and affixed thereto my signature.*

Done at *... this ... day of ... 2005*

[*NAME & SIGNATURE OF FOREIGN MINISTER*]

7. 6   Letter of Accreditation

Accreditation is a formal letter signed by the Minister of Foreign Affairs as proof that a person attending a Conference is duly authorized to participate at the meeting as a true Representative of his country. The letter is usually addressed to the Head of the Organization hosting the Conference such as the Director General of the World Health Organization (WHO). Depending on the Conference's *Rules of Procedure*, delegates may be required to produce their Letters of Accreditation or *Credentials* before they are admitted.

The format of a Letter of Accreditation may vary widely, but its basic components are easy to recognize, namely:

(i)   Introduction of the delegate or delegates,
(ii)   Statement that the delegates are authorized to represent their country at the conference,

(iii)   A plea that they be accorded courtesies deserving of persons of similar status attending the conference to enable them participate effectively in the conference activities, and

(iv)   Name and signature of the Minister for Foreign Affairs.

The following is an example of a Letter of Accreditation:

> *[Name and Address of Head of the Organization]*
> *[Hosting the Conference]*
>
> *I, [name of Minister for Foreign Affairs] of the [name of country] HEREBY AUTHORISE [name and designation of the delegate] to take his seat on the [name of Conference] holding in [place of Conference] for the months of. .... 2006 as Accredited Representative of the Government of . . .*
>
> *Kindly accord him the necessary assistance to enable him, participate effectively in all aspects of the meetings of the [name of Conference] on behalf of the Government of [name of sending State] Done at [capital city of sending State] this . . . day of . . . (month) . . . 2006*
>
> *[NAME OF MINISTER OF FOREIGN AFFAIRS]*
>
> *The following is another example of a Letter of Accreditation:*
> *[NAME AND ADDRESS OF HEAD OF [ORGANIZATION HOSTING THE CONFERENCE]*
>
> *I have the pleasure to inform you that the following persons will represent [name of country] at the [name of conference] holding at [place of meeting] from [date of conference]:*
>
> *[List of the delegation beginning with the Leader of the Delegation]*
>
> *I shall be grateful if you would accord the members of the delegation appropriate courtesies due to them as accredited Representatives of [name of country] as may be necessary to facilitate their effective participation in all aspects of the work of the Conference.*
>
> *[NAME AND SIGNATURE]*
> *[OF MINISTER OF FOREIGN AFFAIRS]*

8

Basic Correspondence on Arrival at Post

8.1 Letter to announce arrival at post

When a new Ambassador, Chargé d'Affaires *en titre* or Acting High Commissioner *en titre* (who has been appointed as substantive Head of Mission) arrives at post to take up his duties, he or she is usually met by the Chief of Protocol of the receiving State. The new Head of Mission is expected to immediately inform the host Minister of Foreign Affairs of his arrival and request an appointment so that he may call on him and, according to the practice in a number of countries, present him with a copy of his *Credentials* or Letter of Introduction as the case may be.

In some countries, the new Head of Mission, if he were an Ambassador, would deliver the copy of his *credentials* to the host Foreign Minister through the Chief of Protocol who receives him on arrival. The letter announcing the ambassador's arrival would take this form:

> Sir,
> *I have the honour to inform you of my arrival in (name of capital city or country) on (date of arrival) in order to take up my duties as Ambassador of (name of the sending State) to (name of the receiving State).*
>
> *I should appreciate it if arrangements could be made for me to call on the appropriate Ministers and senior officials of the Ministry of Foreign Affairs, and in due course, for me to have an Audience with (name of receiving Head of State) for the presentation of my Credentials, the Working Copy of which I enclose herewith.*

With the assurance of my highest consideration,

I have the honour to be, Sir,
Your Obedient Servant,

> *[NAME AND SIGNATURE]*
> *[HAVE AMBASSADOR-designate]*

[NAME AND ADDRESS OF MINISTER]
[OF FOREIGN AFFAIRS OF RECEIVING STATE]

8. 2   Letter to Announce Assumption of Duty

Soon after the presentation of his/her *Letters of Credence* to the President or Minister of Foreign Affairs as the case may be, the new Head of Mission should as soon as possible, inform Heads of Mission accredited to the host country that he/she has presented his letters of credence and that, during his tenure, he would work with them to further the cordial relations that exist between their respective missions and countries. This is an important ritual, which helps the new envoy gain the friendship of other Heads of Mission and indeed, the diplomatic corps. The standard form of such correspondence is as follows:

> *Excellency,*
> *I have the honour to inform you that I have today, 22 July 2005 presented to (Name and title), President of the Republic of (Name of country) my Letter of Credence accrediting me as Ambassador Extraordinary and Plenipotentiary of the Federal Republic of (name of sending state) to the Republic of (name of receiving State).*
>
> *On assuming my duty, I look forward to entering into official and personal contacts with you to further the cordial relations, which happily exist between our two missions and countries.*
>
> *Please accept, Excellency, the assurances of my highest consideration.*

[NAME AND USUAL SIGNATURE]
[OF THE NEW HEAD OF MISSION.]

[NAME AND TITLE OF THE ADDRESSEE]
[ADDRESS OF THE MISSION]

8.3   Acknowledgment of Letter Announcing Assumption of Duty

Heads of Mission are expected to respond promptly to a letter from a new colleague announcing his presentation of credentials and assumption of duty.   Most of them usually do so, but there are quite a few who take this obligation for granted. It is hardly diplomatic to ignore such a correspondence, especially coming from a new Head of Mission who desires to get acquainted as early as possible, with older members of the diplomatic corps.

The following is the standard format of correspondence to acknowledge a letter announcing the presentation of Letters of Credence and assumption of duty:

> *Excellency,*
> *I have the honour to acknowledge receipt of your letter dated 22 July 2005 informing me that you had on that day presented to the ....of the Republic of ...the Letters of ... accrediting you as ... of (name of sending State) to the Republic of (name of receiving)*
> *In expressing my sincere congratulations and best wishes, I would like to assure you that I too look forward to entering into official and personal relationships with you and to further strengthening the friendly ties which so happily exist between our two missions and countries.*
> *Please accept, Excellency and dear Colleague, the assurances of my highest consideration.*
>
> **Name and Signature of Head of Mission]**
> **[Name and Address of new Head of Mission]**

In general, Heads of Mission are faithful with the first paragraph of the correspondence from a new member of the diplomatic corps announcing the presentation of his *Letters of Credence* and assumption of duty. But they take great liberty in composing the second paragraph.

Here are some examples:

(a)

Excellency,

I have the honour to acknowledge receipt of your letter dated 22 July 2005 informing me that you had, on that day, presented to the (Name of Minister of Receiving State) the Letter of Introduction /Letter of Credence accrediting you as Acting High Commissioner/Chargé d'Affaires of the (Name of Sending State) to (Name of Receiving State).

I sincerely desire to maintain and strengthen the ties of friendship, which so happily exist between our two countries and Missions and look forward with pleasure to entering into friendly relations, both official and personal with you.

Please accept, Excellency, the assurances of my highest consideration.

[Name and Signature of the Head of Mission]

(b)

Your Excellency,

I have the honour to acknowledge receipt of your letter dated 22 July 2005, by which you informed me that you had, on that day, presented to the Minister of Foreign Affairs of (Name of Receiving State) the Letter of Introduction/Letter of Credence accrediting you as Acting High Commissioner/Chargé d'Affaires en titre of (Name of Sending State) to (Name of Receiving State).

I wish to reciprocate your kind desire to maintain and strengthen the friendly relations, which so happily exist between our two Countries and Missions.

[NAME AND SIGNATURE OF HEAD OF MISSION]
[NAME AND ADDRESS OF ADDRESSEE]

9

Miscellaneous Communication

In addition to the forms of correspondence that we have discussed in the preceding chapters, diplomats, and indeed public officers, are frequently required to prepare other types of specialized documents. They include *Talking Points, Communiqués, Council Memos, Accessions,* etc. Let us now look at some of them in detail:

9.1   Talking Points

As the name suggests, 'Talking Points' are a set of key points that the participant at a meeting or conference is expected to discuss. There are individuals who attend bilateral or multilateral meetings without an idea of the specific points they would argue or what response they would provide to the proposals of the other party or parties. Well-written 'talking points' can save you or the leader of your delegation the awful embarrassment that would arise from inadequate preparation for important official engagements, especially where exchange of views on bilateral or multilateral issues would be raised.

Suppose your Foreign Minister is scheduled to receive a delegation of the European Union. Your first thought would be to prepare a *specific* or *general* brief on your country's relations with the EU, depending on whether or not you already know the subject matter of the audience.

A brief is said to be 'specific' if the delegation has already communicated the purpose of the meeting. In this case, your brief would zero in on the subject matter. On the other hand, a general brief is one in which the subject matter of the meeting is unknown. You'd then have to speculate on the purpose of the meeting.

Specific or general, a brief has its limitations. Unlike *Talking Points*, the format of a standard brief makes it less easy to use during discussions. This is especially true of newly appointed non-career Foreign Ministers and Ambassadors who might not be conversant with the core issues at stake in relations between the parties.

For all practical purposes, *Talking Points* should serve as a complement of a brief. While the brief provides an overview of the current state of relations between the parties, *Talking Points* help the speaker to see the two sides of the coin at a glance. Put differently, the format of *Talking Points* allows the speaker to know his response to a specific argument or proposal of the other party.

In a general sense therefore, *Talking Points* serve as a useful guide for speakers in terms of *what to say* and *when to say it* in bilateral and multilateral settings. A standard format of *Talking Points* has five main parts, namely: Title, Introduction, Substantive Issues and Conclusion. Using the above analogy of the Foreign Minister and the EU Delegation, our *Talking Points* may take this form:

EU DELEGATION TO PAY A COURTESY CALL
ON THE HONOURABLE MINISTER, 10 FEBRUARY 2009

Talking Points
Introduction
A Delegation of the EU is scheduled to pay a courtesy call on the Honourable Minister on Monday, 10 February 2009. The specific purpose of the visit has not been made known to the Ministry. Honourable Minister may therefore, wish to note for guidance the following points covering the current state of our relations with the European Union:

2. Substantive Issues
(i) Bilateral Political Relations
Relations between our country and the European Union are good.
- 6-8 May 2006: The EU President paid a three-day working visit to our country. During the visit, both sides signed a Memorandum of Understanding on Mutual Cooperation;

- 15 October, 2007: The EU voted against a motion at the United General Assembly to compel our country to surrender all political fugitives in our land;
- 13 June 2004: The EU Parliament voted unanimously in favour of our country's peacekeeping efforts in Africa and called on its member States to increase the current level of assistance.

Honourable Minister may wish to acknowledge these kind gestures and assure the Delegation that our country values its relations with the EU.

(ii) Economic Relations
(a) Since the return of democratic governance to our country, the EU member States have increased their level of investment by 25 percent:

- According to the Central Bank Report of 17 January 2006, the value of total investment from EU member States in our country rose to $8 billion in December 2004 from a paltry $1.5 billion between 1993-1987 during the military regime;

Honourable Minister may wish to acknowledge the rise in investment from member States of the EU since the return of democracy to our country as an expression of confidence in our economy and political stability. The EU should urge the industrialized nations to do the same and invest in our country.

(b) On 13 April 2006, the EU Ministers of Finance rejected debt the rescheduling proposals from Heavily Indebted Countries (HIC).
- The EU Finance Ministers gave two conditions for debt rescheduling: corruption must be reduced by 86 percent per annum and 75 percent of all State revenue must be applied to poverty alleviation programs in a transparent manner.

Honourable Minister may wish to remind the Delegation that it would be a pipe dream to expect the HICs to eliminate corruption and poverty now or in the near future unless the industrialized nations acted quickly to cancel, or at least reschedule, their foreign debts.

(iii)   Human Rights

Dr Gyn Forster, Head of the EU Commission for Human Rights, will be leading the Delegation. Although the visit is supposed to be a courtesy call, it is not unlikely that the Delegation would raise the issue of the 10 Homosexuals who were recently sentenced to death by hanging:

On 13 January 2005, the Court of Appeal upheld the death sentence on 10 homosexuals and rapists by a Lagos High Court. European political leaders and media have been critical of our Court's decision on the matter. The Delegation may therefore attempt to persuade the Federal Government to commute the death sentences to prison terms;

Honourable Minister may wish to inform the Delegation that homosexuality and violent assault on women are classified in our Statute Books as crimes against humanity and the penalty is death. The decision of the Court in the matter is final.

(iv)   Technical Cooperation

The EU has been supportive of our electoral process since 2005:

20 October 2006: The EU donated 500 vote counting machines to the Federal Government. It is expected that the machines would help to reduce vote rigging in the forthcoming General elections;

Honourable Minister may wish to acknowledge this gesture and assure the Delegation that our country is determined to ensure that the forthcoming election must be free and fair.

(v)   Consular Matters

Five   illegal immigrants of African descent died in police custody on 17 July 2006 while awaiting deportation from (name of country). The African Union has made a formal protest to the Presidency of the EU, calling for a thorough investigation into the matter.

The Delegation will be expected to argue that the dead persons were drug traffickers who committed the crime for fear they would face public execution if they returned to their home countries.

> Honourable Minister may wish to inform the delegation that the harassment of peoples of African descent in Europe is unacceptable to this Administration. Accordingly, Honourable Minister may wish to request the assistance of the delegation to investigate the exact status of the dead men and the circumstances of their death.

3. Conclusion

Honourable Minister may wish to conclude by expressing his appreciation for the visit. Our country and the EU have a long history of cooperation in political, economic, cultural and educational fields.

> Honourable Minister may seize the opportunity to discuss the core programs of the present Administration and finally, express the desire of this Administration to work with the EU to expand economic cooperation, so that the concept of globalization would become meaningful to all nations.

Notice that in the above hypothetical example, I have tried to be as specific as possible. Notice also that the points the Minister would be expected to make have been highlighted to enhance legibility.

Talking Points should be typed in large font, preferably font 16 and double space. The font size may be increased even further if the vision quality of the person using the *Talking Points* cannot be trusted!

Talking Points should contain facts and figures, clearly stated and in a few words. It is no place for generalization and ambiguity. Remember the principle of evidence: If you don't provide the facts, the other side would think you're either ignorant of the current issues at stake or poorly prepared for the meeting.

Finally, you should pay attention to the structure of Talking Points:
- State the issue with facts and figures;
- Present the possible argument of the other side; and
- State the policy of your government on the subject.

The format of *Talking Points* may vary considerably from country to country or even within the same Ministry or department. However, the bottom line is that Talking Points must be structured in such a way that the user should be able to *see at a glance* what he or she is expected to say in response to the argument or position of the other party in relation to the specific issues.

9.2   Documents Relating to Treaties

The Vienna Convention on the Law of Treaties of 25 May 1969 defines 'treaty' as "an international agreement concluded between States in written form and governed by international law, whether embodied in a single instrument or in two or more related instruments whatever its particular designation." But this definition has its limitation: First, Treaties can be concluded by non-State actors such as International Organizations. And second, Treaties need not appear in written form before they can be enforced under international law.

However, for the purpose of this book, we would define Treaty as an Agreement in writing between two or more States or International Organizations, formally signed by Representatives and usually *ratified* by the lawmaking authorities of the contracting States. Indeed, a treaty is a legal instrument by which the contracting parties (States or International Organizations) commit themselves to undertake certain obligations as specified under the existing treaty.

A Treaty may be bilateral (i.e. between two States) or multilateral (i.e. among several States or International Organizations). Although legal experts usually draft Treaty and treaty-related documents, diplomats should acquire the skill for drafting such simple instruments as *Full Powers*, Ratification, *Adherence* and Accession, as the case may be.   In addition, it is important that diplomats are able to recognize those instruments that are usually signed by Heads of State, Ministers of Foreign Affairs or some other authorized entity.

(a) Ratification

Ratification, as Ernest Satow rightly observes, "is a solemn act by which a Sovereign or President of a Republic declares that a treaty, convention or other international instruments has been submitted to him and that, after examining it, he has given his approval thereto and undertaken its complete and faithful observance." Put differently, ratification is a process by which nations reconfirm their consent to be bound by the terms of a treaty.

The act of signing a treaty by Plenipotentiaries, that is persons vested with full powers to act on behalf of their governments, does not in itself constitute a final commitment of a country to be bound by the treaty. Most multilateral treaties and important bilateral agreements usually contain a clause to the effect that the treaty shall not bind the contracting parties until a further process of confirmation has been completed. That is to say, the plenipotentiaries sign the agreement with a *subject to ratification* clause. Ratification gives the contracting parties a second chance to review the terms of the treaty to ensure they are fully aware of their obligations under the treaty.

Ratification may be signed by Heads of State, Foreign Ministers or some other authorized persons, depending on the degree of importance attached to the treaty by the contracting parties. And in general, the ratification of most important treaties requires the approval of the country's Legislature.

The following is a format of an *Instrument of Ratification* signed by a Head of State:

> **Instrument of Ratification of the Treaty Between (Names of the Contracting Parties) On (Subject of the Treaty)**
>
> **Whereas** a Treaty on the (subject of the Treaty) was signed between (name of Contracting Parties) in (name of place) on (date of signature);
>
> **And Whereas** it is provided in (relevant Article) of the aforesaid Treaty that the Treaty is subject to ratification by both States and that the Instrument of Ratification shall be registered with the (name of place of Registration or deposit of instrument of Ratification);
>
> **And Whereas** the Government of (Name of country ratifying The Treaty) has, by a decision duly reached in accordance with its Constitutional processes, agreed to ratify the aforesaid Treaty.
>
> **Now Therefore**, I (name of Head of State and official Designation) do hereby ratify the aforesaid Treaty.
>
> **In Witness Whereof**, I have hereunto set my hand and caused the Seal of (name of country ratifying the treaty) to be affixed to these Presents.

> **Done at** *(Place of Ratification) this.....Day of.........in the year ...*
> [Name and Signature of Head of State]

(b) Certificate of Exchange

In the above example, the Treaty provides that the Instrument of Ratification shall be registered with a designated Authority, which may be the Secretary General of the United Nations or the Secretariat of an Organization to which the Contracting Parties belong. However, there are occasions when Instruments of Ratification may simply be *exchanged* between the parties and registration may not be required. This act of exchanging the Instruments of Ratification constitutes ratification in itself and it is recorded in what is known as a *Certificate of Exchange*.

The following is the format of a *Certificate of Exchange* which records the Ratification of a bilateral Treaty signed by Foreign Ministers on behalf of their governments:

> **The Undersigned** *having met together for the purpose of Exchanging the Instruments of Ratification of an Agreement for (Subject of the Treaty) which was signed at (Place and date) by Representatives of the Government of ... and the Government of; and the respective Ratifications of the said Agreement having been found in good and due form, the said Exchange took place this day.*
>
> **In Witness Whereof,** *the Undersigned have signed the present Certificate.*
>
> **Done** *in duplicate at (Place of Exchange) this ...day of (month and year).*
>
> *[SIGNATURES]*
>
> *Notice that the above format may be adapted to reflect the status of the person having full powers to exchange the Instrument of Ratification.*

(c) Joint Communiqué

A Communiqué is usually a brief statement issued at the end of a conference for *public information*. It contains the highlight of decisions taken at the conference. Communiqués are a common feature of meetings of Heads of State and Government or Summits. In some instances however, a communiqué may be as elaborate as the full report of a summit. This is true of Communiqués released at the end of summits of African Heads of State and Government.

Whether long or short, the format of a communiqué is simple. It contains five distinct parts, namely: title, preamble, list of participants, substantive issues, appreciation or vote of thanks, closing, date and venue of next meeting.

While it would be desirable to re-invent the wheel, you don't have all the time to do so immediately after a summit of Heads of State. You are therefore better off grabbing the Communiqué issued at the end of any State Visit to your country and adapting your present task to the format. But you must be careful when adapting your work not to copy irrelevances not appropriate or suitable to the particular Summit you are dealing with!

10

Performance Measurement in Diplomatic Systems

10.1 Foreign Ministries in the face of Change

In the preceding chapters, we examined the common forms of diplomatic correspondence in use in most diplomatic services. We noted that although the format of the correspondence may vary from country to country, the thrust of diplomatic correspondence is usually the same: to communicate thought in an elegant, unambiguous and if necessary, memorable language. But because it takes effort and commitment on the part of diplomats to achieve this goal, most diplomatic systems have developed specific measures to persuade their officials in the Ministries of Foreign Affairs (MFAs) and their Missions overseas to recognize competence in diplomatic communication as an important tool for performance measurement. So, in this chapter, we will examine some of the methods that have been adopted in some advanced countries to measure and improve performance among their diplomats to meet national objectives.

Indeed, the question of performance measurement in Ministries of Foreign Affairs has been the preoccupation of career diplomats and scholars over the last three decades or so. In a recent major contribution to this subject, former Indian Ambassador and diplomacy scholar, Prof. Kishan S. Rana discussed different models of Performance Management in MFAs which have put to question our old assumption that performance of diplomatic activities can neither be quantified nor measured (Rana, July 2004).

The end of the Cold War in 1990 and the rapid pace of globalization created new dynamics that have tended to challenge our traditional notion of diplomacy and the role of diplomats in global politics. In most countries for example, the management of international relations is no longer the prerogative of the MFAs as multiple actors have intruded into the scene. In the some of the developing countries, there are even parallel department and Ministries that compete with and sometimes successfully outdo the MFAs in the policy formulation and management of international relations.

What is more disturbing is that MFAs in developing countries have been unsuccessful in shielding themselves from the wave of public service reform that have been sweeping across the world since the past 30 years. These reforms have taken the form of application of corporate management style to the management of foreign affairs, budget cuts, reduction of number of resident diplomatic missions abroad and the increasing adoptions of other measures to ensure diplomatic representation from Headquarters. The purpose of all these reforms is the ensure value for money and apply limited financial resources of the state in a manner to provide for the need of the majority of the people.

The Ministries of Foreign Affairs are in a special vulnerable position. Much of the work they do is outside the immediate perception of the general public, including those in national parliament who have powers to take decisions that affect the service. And we have energetically defended the position that our work cannot be measured, and in some cases, we have taken it to mean a pretext for inactivity! There was the story of an eminent ambassador of the former Soviet Union who was introduced to a farmer in the countryside. The farmer replied, and quiet honestly, "But what does he do?"

With the exception of consular work of Missions and protocol related services, the general public in most developing countries is unaware of the *raison d'etre* of their countries diplomatic representation overseas. But ignorance of the work of diplomatic missions is not limited to the ordinary folks as one would imagine. For example, this author was shocked when a few years ago, an aspirant to the presidency of Nigeria was asked what his priorities would be if he was elected President. He replied, without equivocation, "I will close down most of the Nigerian diplomatic Missions abroad!"

Perhaps the presidential aspirant would have been concerned with how best to use the nations diplomatic instrument to achieve such high national goals as economic promotion, foreign direct investment and peaceful coexistence with neighbors. But he would have none of that. Close down the Missions!!!

The above observation may appear exceptional, coming from a high profile figure who would have been President of the Federal Republic of Nigeria. But the statement is indicative of the vulnerability of the Ministries of Foreign Affairs in the global trend and the challenge they face in most countries.

Limited knowledge of the work of diplomatic missions in the developing countries has meant that MFAs end up becoming the whipping boys of troubled fiscal policies at home. When it comes to budgetary allocation, the Ministries of Foreign Affairs usually get the shorter end of the stick because most legislators are not convinced that the diplomatic service should be one of the immediate priorities of government.

Yet the negative perception of the diplomatic service as an unnecessary drain of public resources is happening at a time when the demand for an assertive foreign policy is greatest and public expectations from the diplomatic missions are highest. But there's one solution MFAs must strengthen their mechanisms to monitor and enforce performance at home and abroad as well as strengthen their tools of public diplomacy.

10.2 Framework of Performance Measurement

Measuring the performance of diplomats can be assessed in terms of the expected role of a country's Embassies or High Commissions overseas, the quality of human resource development and training of the diplomatic system and the capacity of MFAs to provide public outreach for the work of the diplomatic service as a whole.

10.3 Target Setting for Missions Abroad

The diplomatic system has two sides: the Ministry of Foreign Affairs sometimes referred as 'Headquarters' and its network of diplomatic Missions abroad, known variously as embassies or high commissions. The Consulates General also form part of a nation's diplomatic service although their functions are not classified as strictly diplomatic under the Vienna Convention the embassies, high commissions and consulates represent the field units of the diplomatic system and their relationship with the MFAs must be such as to ensure an effective performance of the system.

It is one thing to have a foreign policy. It is another thing to have an effective mechanism for the implementation of this foreign policy. As one diplomacy scholar put it beautifully, "Ensuring that the country has the best possible mechanism for advancing its external interests is a public good, and a factor of basic good governance. It does not suffice that a country should have a foreign policy that best serves its interest. It must also have the optimal ground mechanism to implement this policy and to build and operate the external relationships that best serve its interests." (Rana, 2005 p.4).

10.4 Structure of MFAs

Traditionally, MFAs are divided in Directorates sometimes referred to as Territorial Divisions in some countries such as the Indian Foreign Service. In Nigeria, the territorial divisions correspond to the Directorate system. In the case of multilateral responsibilities, the Directorate of International Organizational covers such multilateral institutions as the United Nations, the Commonwealth and related bodies such as the G 77 etc. Regional organizations such as the Economic Community of West African States (ECOWAS) and the African Union have separate departments, thereby underscoring the importance of these bodies in the foreign policy calculation of Nigeria.

The Directorates have responsibility to supervise the activities of the embassies, high commissions and Permanent Missions that deal with issues concerning them. In some countries, the MFAs, in collaboration with the Territorial Divisions or Directorates determine the targets for each Missions and together both the Missions and MFAs establish the basis of meeting those targets and by implication, the framework for measuring the degree of their performance or otherwise.

Indeed, most countries establish diplomatic missions to achieve well-defined national objectives which correspond to their national interest. This is especially true of such countries as United States, the United Kingdom, France, China, Canada, Singapore, Germany, Japan, Australia, New Zealand, etc. An ambassador or other classes of Heads of Mission such as Charge d' Affaires *en titre* receive targets that they are expected to address in their respective Missions or Posts as the case may be. In France, this document is known as 'ambassador's instructions' while in the United States, it is known as Mission's Action Program. In other countries the 'ambassador's instruction' may take different names. But the unifying element is that they all represent what headquarters expects the Mission to accomplish within a given timeframe, usually one year. Once a target has been set for the Head of Mission and his or her team, it becomes easier to monitor performance on the basis of the target. And usually the quality and quantity of the Mission's correspondence with Headquarters or reportage is the easiest way to measure performance.

It has been observed that most developing countries do not seem to take foreign policy seriously. Missions are established without deliberate effort to identify and articulate specific national objectives and what the resident diplomatic Mission is expected to achieve. They seem to establish diplomatic Missions as a reciprocal gesture of friendly relations between Heads of State with little or no sense of what the mission can contribute to national development. In some instances, new Heads of Mission do not receive any specific instructions as to what they are expected to achieve. Sometimes, the MFA officials believe that the ambassador has got enough experience and does not require further instructions. They believe that the ambassador has got enough experience to know what he is expected to do or to look for in his country of accreditation. In other words, the new Head of Mission is left to sort himself out and if he lacks experience and imagination, his tour of duty will turn out to be a disaster for the Mission and his country.

The result of this attitude towards the diplomatic process is the frequent complaints by the media and even some segments of the national leadership that the diplomatic missions are a drain of the scarce resource of the nation. The resident ambassador in turn considers that non-performance is an option, since in this case, he had not received written targets to achieve and there is even no obvious mechanism to monitor and enforce performance. In the end, it is a lose-lose situation for the country. But this does not have to be so because diplomacy is a critical tool for national development when understood and applied in the manner of the founding fathers on this noble profession.

10.5 The Singapore Experience

Singapore is one of the few countries that have shown that diplomatic relations must serve as a mechanism to advance national strategic and economic objectives. In Singapore, new heads of Mission receive a form of annual action plan, showing what the nation's expectations are in that particular country or region. Singapore has developed a unique format for monitoring compliance with set targets. The Singapore method takes the form of a monthly reporting format divided into three parts: the first part shows the major activities performed by mission within the period; the second part requires the mission to indicate the major dispatches and reports that had been sent to headquarters by the individual officers of the mission and the Head of Mission; and thirdly, the Mission is expected to list new contacts that the Mission had established with influential authorities in the host country. As Prof. Ranna suggested, this method is worthy of emulation by developing countries who have not yet grasped the essence of the diplomatic enterprise.

10.6 Quantifying Diplomatic Tasks

Can we measure or assign monetary value to most common diplomatic tasks just as one would do to, say the number of customer a bank official is able to recruit in a month or the number of foreign companies a mission is able to persuade to invest in one's country?

This author has had the opportunity to participate in workshops where the focus of debate was the difficulty of measuring or quantifying diplomatic tasks. I recall that several years ago, the performance of a Nigerian Head of Mission was measured against the number of foreign investments he was able to bring into his country. This policy was not followed to the end, apparently because of the realization that the nature of the domestic political situation has a lot to do with the decision of foreign investors to accept one country instead of the other as an investment destination.

But regardless of the difficulty of assigning monetary value to a number of diplomatic tasks, with the exception of basic consular functions such as issuance of passport and visas and related travel documents, the incompetence of diplomatic Missions should not be protected under the pretext that diplomatic functions cannot be measured or quantified. On the contrary, the performance of Missions can be assessed with a variety of methods that have been developed by MFAs in a number of countries.

10.7 "Using Writing Skill to Measure Performance"

We have noted earlier in this book that most diplomatic functions are expressed in writing. A simple method to measure the performance of diplomatic missions from headquarters is to use the written communication skill of the Heads of Mission and his team. For example, MFAs can assign their Missions can demand that their Missions submit not less than five Chancery Reports to Headquarters in a month and Head of Mission must render a dispatch every month to the Minister of Foreign Affairs. Heads of Mission and their teams should not be restricted in terms of the subject matter of the Chancery Reports and Dispatches as long as the issues covered are relevant to the diplomatic objectives of the Mission and consistent with the country's national interest.

10.8 *Quality of Leadership in MFAs*

For the above measure to work effectively, the caliber of leadership at MFAs from the Minister to the Directorate level must be such as to command the respect of the officers in the Missions. The diplomat overseas will be motivated to write if he is certain that the persons who will have to read his reports at Headquarters are persons who are competent and knowledgeable to offer even the minimum of intelligent comments on the substance of his report. Think of a case when a Head of Mission writes a dispatch to his Minister only to receive an acknowledgement which has no bearing whatsoever to the substance of the dispatch itself. At best, the diplomat will draw the unhappy conclusion that the leadership of his supervising ministry did not read the report. This is a clever way to kill incentive and encourage the Head of Mission not even bother to write again.

10.9 *Quality of Relationship of MFAs and Missions*

The quality of relationship between MFAs and the field missions is also essential to bring out the best of both worlds. In some of the less developed diplomatic systems, the relationship between MFAs and their missions overseas is so acrimonious that routine correspondence from Missions is hardly acknowledged, talk less take required action on them. In societies where the larger society has been polarized along ethnic or tribal lines, some heads of departments have a tendency to identify the ethnic origin of the Head of Mission in a given country before deciding how to respond to his request. As in the previous example, a strong leadership in the MFAs is essential to discourage the persistence of attitudes that kill incentive of diplomats at Missions overseas and encourage them to live up to their expectation in terms of meeting their set targets in the Mission's plan action programme.

10.10 The Inspection System

The Inspection system in MFAs still remains the most common form of performance evaluation in most countries. In the advanced nations, the system is being replaced with other more sophisticated methods that respond to the modern technologies in the market. In some countries such as Germany, there is an attempt to integrate the Foreign Ministry with the overseas missions which makes the existence of territorial divisions or Directorates superfluous. But for most of the developing world, Foreign Service Inspection will remain with us for years to come in spite its limitations to effectively impact on performance of the system.

Indeed, the Foreign Service Inspection has generally focused on issues of administrative character such as discipline, Foreign Service rules and regulations, financial management, consular matters, local staff etc. There has been little or no concern for purely diplomatic functions of Missions to determine the degree of effectiveness of officials to meet the set targets for the mission in terms of reportage, specific measures to improve bilateral relations, representational duties, economic diplomacy, and contact with upcoming local personages and consular issues.

10.11 Reforming the Inspectional System

Clearly the Foreign Service Inspection system must be adapted to meet the challenge of the diplomatic enterprise in the 21st Century. The officials assigned to Inspection of Missions must be persons who are considered by their peers as outstanding. They must be sound and motivated individuals, possessing written and verbal communication skills that can command the respect of their colleagues overseas. Less competent officials should be kept out of the Inspection process because they bring their prejudices to the scheme and can hardly command the respect of their colleagues.

In the longer term, developing countries may consider the creation of independent Inspectorate system outside the Ministry of Foreign Affairs as in the United States and Germany. As Prof. Rana observed (July 2004), the US State Department operates a large Inspection network, headed by an Inspector General, Deputy Inspector General, Senior Inspectors and Inspectors who visit every embassy once three years. Similarly, the German Foreign Office has an Inspectors General assisted by two deputies who travel round the world on inspection duties. Six months prior to the inspection, the embassy concerned endorses to the Inspection Unit all its outbound correspondence and reportage. These correspondence are in turn closely analyzed to determine the quality of reportage and responsiveness to different stakeholders. It was also reported that Brazil, China, Egypt, France, Russia and the UK among others use comparable inspection methodology to measure the competence level of their overseas Missions.

The use of an Inspectorate regime that is independent or semi-independent of the MFA apparatus has the merit of overcoming the shortcomings of the MFA Inspection system where human weaknesses interfere with the need for objective criteria in performance evaluation. Some countries, as indicated above are already experimenting with independent Inspection system which should be emulated by developing nations that aspire to build a strong and effective diplomatic system.

10.12   Quality of Human Resource Development

The quality of the human resource management in MFAs represent the most important assets of the diplomatic service of nations. Every effort must therefore be made to shield this critical mass from tendencies to undermine commitment to achieving the diplomatic objectives of the Ministry and country. There are four ways of looking at the human resource dimension of the diplomatic system, namely, recruitment and promotion procedures as well as training and welfare requirements of the diplomatic personnel.

10.12.1 Recruitment

The rapid changes in the international environment within the past few decades have thrown up new subject areas and challenges that today's diplomats must have to adapt to acquire the necessary competences to meet the new skill levels demanded by the new environment. Although the diplomat does not need to be an expert in all the subject areas, he or she must be knowledgeable enough to understand the issues and report outcomes to his home government in an intelligible manner. The quality of new entrants to the diplomatic service is therefore essential to ensure that new diplomats have the initial preparation for the challenges of the job. In most European, American and Asia diplomatic services, the qualification for entry into the service is rigorous and tedious. New entrants are expected to take written and oral examinations, besides the general requirement for entry into the Public Service.

In Nigeria, the system of recruitment into the Ministry of Foreign Affairs appears to have been streamlined since the past two decades or so, in the sense that all new entrants to the service are bright young men and women with the potential to rise to ambassadorial level in the future. This is good for the future of the Nigerian diplomacy. But this happy development was not like that in the past. The practice was to convert persons who didn't posses university education to the diplomatic cadre after years in the administrative branch also known as executive cadre. This practice tended to dilute the quality of the diplomatic corps as well as dampen the morale of those officers who had sacrificed otherwise promising academic career in the universities to join the diplomatic service in the expectation that the Foreign Service would offer them the opportunity to apply the skills they had acquired through higher education.

As would be expected, the conversation system bred divisions, envy and jealousy as high performers and the non-performers were regrettably placed under the same roof with no system of reward for outstanding performance and competence. Besides, all class of officials ran the same promotion schedules based on seniority. The result of this mixed grill was that some class of officers spent their lives in purely diplomatic tasks such as political, economic and multilateral responsibilities while others made strenuous efforts to get assigned to non-diplomatic duties including administration and welfare matters.

10.12.2 On promotion

Indeed, the promotion or career advancement of members of the diplomatic service is an important aspect of human resource management which MFAs must take seriously in any attempt to address the issue of performance enhancement in the diplomatic system. Regrettably, as experts have observed, few countries have an official promotion policy that recognizes the high achievers. Instead promotion is based on Seniority which meant that persons recruited into the Foreign Service in a particular period were deemed to have qualified for promotion to the next stage at the same time.

As though to address, at least in part, the concerns of MFA's officials regarding what had been described as the 'conveyor belt' promotion method, the Nigerian Public Service introduced an examination system as a measure to promote efficiency and encourage the higher achievers. But the examination format was criticized for its lack of depth and potential for manipulation.

It is heartening to note that the promotion method for Foreign Service Officers in Nigeria is being reviewed as part of the Reform of the Civil Service. It is hoped that the reform will address the known lapses of the present system to make promotion a credible mechanism for career advancement in the Nigeria Foreign Service.

Nigeria can learn and adapt the practice in some countries where promotion is not seniority-based and automatic. Instead, persons who consider themselves suitable for promotion are required to apply for promotion within a give time period. Such persons are then subjected to rigorous written and oral interviews to determine their suitability for promotion to the next senior grade. MFAs in developing countries should be encouraged to try out such promotion methods that are used in more advanced systems to ensure that persons occupying important positions in their MFAs and Missions abroad are truly persons who enjoy their confidence and respect of their colleagues or peers.

10.13 Models of Reward System for Performance

It has been reported that some countries that tried a reward system to recognize outstanding performances finally dumped the scheme when it was discovered that it bred divisions and apathy within the ranks of MFA officials. The chances of abuse of such a system of reward could be even greater in those developing countries where, more often than not, the loyalty of the MFA's leadership goes first to the Tribe rather than to the diplomatic service. As we have said elsewhere it is important is to ensure that the leadership of MFAs is competent, detribalized and nationalistic. To appoint persons whose first loyalty goes to the Tribe as against the State is not only a recipe to destroy the nation's diplomatic system, but also to create a class of incompetent persons who rely on sycophancy and nepotism as the fastest means of career advancement rather merit.

Singapore has a unique reward system in its public service that can be adapted to suit the practice of other countries (See Rana, July 2004). This method is used for the evaluation of the personnel of the Foreign Ministry. By applying a system known as Current Evaluated Potential (CEP), the government of the Island State is able to anticipate the growth potential of officials who have served between 10 to 20 years. These individuals are then placed notionally at the level they may attain after 25 years of service on the basis of the posts currently available. The CEP rankings are conducted each year, and are not disclosed to the individual concerned, but they form the basis of career planning.

In the United States as in most modern Foreign Ministries, promotion to high positions involves special procedures such as written exams and interviews and careful appraisal of the individual's record. An individual has to apply to open 'promotion window' which has to be entered within six years failing to do so, the individual has to quit. It is also reported that Australia, China and New Zealand among others, require the individuals to apply for a promotion, against vacancies that are available. This is in contrast to the conveyor belt principle mentioned earlier in which promotion to senior grades in the public service is based on seniority.

It all sounds good to have a reward system that encourages performance in the diplomatic system. The application of this principle can be complex in some countries, especially in some developing countries where other non-merit-related criteria such as the ethnic configuration and State of Origin are equally important. In such instances, special care must be taken to ensure that quality of the diplomatic personnel is not undermined in the pursuit of fair representation. With a committed leadership in MFAs, quality and performance can be achieved within the diplomatic system without compromising the principle of fair or equitable representation.

10.14 On Training

Besides the need for an effective promotion system to raise morale and encourage performance among diplomats, the need for constant training of officials should form an important part of the human resources management. The old thinking that necessary diplomatic skills can be accumulated over time is no longer adequate. Most modern Foreign Ministries encourage the training of their officials at the mid-career and senior levels in relevant subject areas to enable them upgrade their skills and keep abreast of developments in other diplomatic services in the world. This should be encouraged as well as collaboration between Foreign Ministries of friendly countries. Such collaboration can be useful to help officials of both countries compare notes and share knowledge and expertise in areas of mutual interest and techniques.

10.15 Welfare and Performance Measurement

Finally, the Welfare of the diplomatic personnel should be seen by governments as a key element of Human Resource development.

Perhaps Singapore offers the best example of the intrinsic relationship between officer's welfare and their performance. It has been widely reported that in Singapore, public officials, including diplomats are among the highest pain in the world. No wonder then that Singaporean diplomats and public officers are also among the most hardworking and competent in the world. Then, contrast the Singapore experience with diplomats from some developing countries in Washington who engage in extra-official duties including taxi service to make ends meet!

The performance level of diplomats can be measured in some specific ways including the use of their written communication output. But they can perform best when the working environment is conducive and resources available and adequate for the day to day operations of the Missions. In addition, promotion arrangements based on credible mechanisms that recognize and reward outstanding performance as well as the establishment of an Independent Inspectorate system to measure the degree of performance on the basis of set targets can be boost to the diplomatic system of any country.

10.16 Performance Evaluation at Headquarters

We have noted above that diplomatic missions abroad are answerable to MFAs in what they do or what they do not do. It follows that for the network of diplomatic missions to be effective, the leadership and personnel at headquarters must also be such as to enjoy the confidence and respect of the officials overseas.

In some developing countries where the level of income in the public service is extremely poor, career diplomats look forward to overseas postings as an escape to heaven. Overseas postings can make a difference between life and death. When they are posted back to headquarters, they spend time planning when to leave on their next overseas' assignment. Rather than apply themselves to do the coordinating work which MFAs are expected to do and give guidance to the missions abroad, some senior officials dispense their energy working to undermine the Missions abroad. Sometimes important correspondence from the Missions are hardly acknowledged and basic information is not even available. Some MFA officials go to the extent of issuing unauthorized instructions to Heads of Mission abroad and even threaten them with 'immediate recall' if they failed to comply with some spurious directives. In some ways, the personnel at headquarters turn themselves into *de facto* dictators believing that they have the supreme powers over the Heads of Mission and their officers abroad! Now, contrast this again with Singapore where the income of Foreign Affairs officials is as high as in the Private Sector so much so that some Singaporean diplomats have little or no incentive to serve abroad!

10.17 Uniform Standards of Performance

The same standards of performance criteria expected of Heads of Missions and their teams should apply to the officials at headquarters. The MFA officials at Headquarters must develop critical writing skill to communicate the content of reports from missions to higher authorities.

As we have noted previously, one serious problem that confronts MFAs all over the world is the public ignorance of the work that

Missions do on behalf of their nations. MFAs have an important role to develop an outreach program otherwise know as *public diplomacy* to explain to the wider audience the nature of the diplomatic enterprise and how, if well managed, can contribute to national development. In some countries, there is a scheduled briefing of the public and media organizations of the achievements of the diplomatic Missions in a given time period, usually on an annual basis. This practice removes the stigma of elitism which over the years has tended to create a hateful divide between MFA officials and their counterpart in the other government services.

In Nigeria, the Ministry of Foreign Affairs established an outreach facility known as the Public Relations and Cultural Unit (PRCU). Like most other divisions of the Ministry, the PRCU must be given recognition as a critical aspect of the diplomatic process to raise the morale of officers deployed to serve in that section. It goes without saying that officials of the PRCU ought to have a chance to participate in external programmes that expose them to current Information and Technology resources. Otherwise, they will continue to regard the Unit as a dumping ground for those who either don't have godfathers or cannot to anything else at headquarters.

In summary, we live in an age when the use of public fund has come increasingly under close scrutiny in most countries. Concepts that were hitherto reserved for the corporate world are now being applied to the public service including the Ministries of Foreign Affairs. The need for officials of Ministries of Foreign Affairs at headquarters and at Missions abroad to justify their work has become imperative. The system of measuring performance must therefore be of continuing interest to the leadership of the MFAs as well as Heads of Mission abroad.

The 21st Century is a century of self-justification for the diplomatic service. Diplomats must cast aside the traditional chains that had prevented them from reaching out to the larger public either in their countries of accreditation or even in their own countries. An eminent Canadian diplomat was reported to have written , "The new diplomacy, as I call it, is to a large extent public diplomacy and requires different skills, techniques and attitudes. Traditional diplomacy I came to understand was a recipe for ineffectiveness. Almost everything I regarded as a qualification was in fact closer to being a hindrance to carrying out my tasks effectively." (Rana, 2005, p. 85).

Public diplomacy which we can approximate to Public Relations provides MFAs and their network of Missions abroad with the opportunity to engage meaningfully with the enlightened public on the nature and scope of their functions. The era of hiding from the public in the name of diplomatic sense of preservation is over. To persevere in that obsolete practice is to write the epitaph of the whole diplomatic system. Heads of Mission must therefore be flexible in the discharge of their functions and the same principle should apply to the leadership of the MFAs at headquarters.

But regardless of the degree of flexibility that Heads of Mission wish to assume, they must consult frequently with the leadership at Headquarters when decisions of high diplomatic significance are at stake. The bottom-line is to give visibility to the diplomatic process, while withholding such information that may be considered inappropriate for public disclosure at a given time.

In the end, the performance of any diplomatic system should be measured in terms of the quality and quantity of written communication between Missions and with Headquarters of the sending and receiving states became diplomacy, after all, is about learning to write well in a special way.

$\boxed{11}$

Concluding Remarks

A few years ago, a retired Nigerian ambassador asked me, ' why don't you write a book on Nigerian Foreign Policy? I replied that perhaps I would do so, but only when new elements have been introduced to enrich the existing literature on our Foreign Policy.

Of course, the average Nigerian diplomat is familiar with public expectations of his role as the country's representative either overseas or even in Abuja, at least in the eyes of the diplomatic community. He is aware of what constitutes our national interest, which, in spite of aggressive competing interests, the Ministry of Foreign Affairs was established to pursue.

But I have come to the conclusion that rather than engage in the rehearsal of Nigeria's national interest, because it is already well-known to all us, it might be more urgent to attempt to equip new and older diplomats with the critical tool to transmit the foreign policy of government. I can be more graphic: If a nation's foreign policy cannot be expressed in writing and correctly too, it will be stillborn. So, in this little book, I have examined in some detail the common forms of diplomatic communication from the seemingly simple letter to acknowledgement of the receipt of correspondence to the more complex correspondence relating to the appointment of Special Envoys.

The good news is that diplomatic correspondence gives us room for adaptation. But that is not say we should take total liberty with the format of diplomatic communication, which, over the centuries, has become something like a sacred art. I should add that those who fail to honour the sanctity of diplomatic correspondence do so to the detriment of their persons and nations.

It is my hope that this book will help diplomats of today and· diplomats of tomorrow not only in Nigeria but also all over the world to better appreciate the uniqueness of our profession and exert their best endeavours to advance the sanctity and dignity of diplomatic correspondence.

Suggestions for further Reading

Berridge, G. R. *Diplomacy: Theory and Practice* (Palgrave: Macmillan), 2002

'Diplomacy,' in *Encyclopedia Britannica* (2001-2003)

'Diplomacy,' in *Encarta Encyclopedia* (2003-2005)

Feltham, R. G., *Diplomatic Handbook* (USA: Addison Wesley Longman), 1998.

Freeman, Charles (ed.), *Diplomat's Dictionary* (Charles Freeman and Company) 1997.

Hocking, Brian (ed.), Foreign *Ministries: Change and Adaptation* (St. Martin's Press), 1999.

Melissen, Jan (ed.), *Innovation in Diplomatic Practice* (Palgrave: Macmillan) 1998.

Rana, Kishan S., *Performance Management in Foreign Ministries*, In Discussion Papers in Diplomacy, Netherlands Institute of Int'l Relations, No. 93, July 2004.

Rana, Kishan S., The 21st Century Ambassador: Plenipotentiary to chief Executive, (New Delhi: Oxford University Press, 2005)

Rana, Kishan S., Inside Diplomacy (Manas, New Delhi, 2002)

Rana, Kishan S., Bilateral Diplomacy (Diplo Projects, Malta, 2002).

Satow, Ernest, A *Guide To Diplomatic Practice* (London: Longmans), 2002

Vienna Convention on Diplomatic Practice, 1961

Vienna Convention on Diplomatic Relations
Done at Vienna on 18 April 1961

The States Parties to the present Convention,

Recalling that peoples of all nations from ancient times have recognized the status of diplomatic agents,

Having in mind the purposes and principles of the Charter of the United Nations concerning the sovereign equality of States, the maintenance of international peace and security, and the promotion of friendly relations among nations,

Believing that an international convention on diplomatic intercourse, privileges and immunities would contribute to the development of friendly relations among nations, irrespective of their differing constitutional and social systems,

Realizing that the purpose of such privileges and immunities is not to benefit individuals but to ensure the efficient performance of the functions of diplomatic missions as representing States,

Affirming that the rules of customary international law should continue to govern questions not expressly regulated by the provisions of the present Convention,

Have agreed as follows:

Article I
For the purpose of the present Convention, the following expressions shall have the meanings hereunder assigned to them:

(a)   the "head of the mission" is the person charged by the sending State with the duty of acting in that capacity;

(b)   the "members of the mission" are the head of the mission and the members of the staff of the mission;

(c)   the "members of the staff of the mission" are the members of the diplomatic staff, of the administrative and technical staff and of the service staff of the mission;

(d)   the "members of the diplomatic staff" are the members of the staff of the mission having diplomatic rank;

(e)   a "diplomatic agent" is the head of the mission or a member of the diplomatic staff of the mission;

(f)   the "members of the administrative and technical staff" are the members of the staff of the mission employed in the administrative and technical service of the mission;

(g)   the "members of the service staff" are the members of the staff of the mission in the domestic service of the mission;

(h)   a "private servant" is a person who is in the domestic service of a member of the mission and who is not an employee of the sending State;

(i)   the "premises of the mission" are the buildings or parts of buildings and the land ancillary thereto, irrespective of ownership, used for the purposes of the mission including the residence of the head of the mission.

Article 2

The establishment of diplomatic relations between States, and of permanent diplomatic missions, takes place by mutual consent.

Article 3

1.   The functions of a diplomatic mission consist inter alia in:

(a)   representing the sending State in the receiving State;

(b)   protecting in the receiving State the interests of the sending State and of its nationals, within the limits permitted by international law;

(c)   negotiating with the Government of the receiving State;

(d)   ascertaining by all lawful means conditions and developments in the receiving State, and reporting thereon to the Government of the sending State;

(e) promoting friendly relations between the sending State and the receiving State, and developing their economic, cultural and scientific relations.

2. Nothing in the present Convention shall be construed as preventing the performance of consular functions by a diplomatic mission.

Article 4
1. The sending State must make certain that the agreement of the receiving State has been given for the person it proposes to accredit as head of the mission to that State.
2. The receiving State is not obliged to give reasons to the sending State for a refusal to grant agreement.

Article 5
1. The sending State may, after it has given due notification to the receiving States concerned, accredit a head of mission or assign any member of the diplomatic staff, as the case may be, to more than one State, unless there is express objection by any of the receiving States.
2. If the sending State accredits a head of mission to one or more other States it may establish a diplomatic mission headed by a "chargé d'affaires" ad interim in each State where the head of mission has not his permanent seat.
3. A head of mission or any member of the diplomatic staff of the mission may act as representative of the sending State to any international organization.

Article 6
Two or more States may accredit the same person as head of mission to another State, unless objection is offered by the receiving State.

Article 7
Subject to the provisions of Articles 5, 8, 9 and 11, the sending State may freely appoint the members of the staff of the mission. In the case of military, naval or air attaches, the receiving State may require their names to be submitted beforehand, for its approval.

Article 8

1.   Members of the diplomatic staff of the mission should in principle be of the nationality of the sending State.
2.   Members of the diplomatic staff of the mission may not be appointed from among persons having the nationality of the receiving State, except with the consent of that State which may be withdrawn at any time.
3.   The receiving State may reserve the same right with regard to nationals of a third State who are not also nationals of the sending State.

Article 9

1.   The receiving State may at any time and without having to explain its decision, notify the sending State that the head of the mission or any member of the diplomatic staff of the mission is persona non grata or that any other member of the staff of the mission is not acceptable. In any such case, the sending State shall, as appropriate, either recall the person concerned or terminate his functions with the mission. A person may be declared non grata or not acceptable before arriving in the territory of the receiving State.
2.   If the sending State refuses or fails within a reasonable period to carry out its obligations under paragraph 1 of this Article, the receiving State may refuse to recognize the person concerned as a member of the mission.

Article 10

1.   The Ministry for Foreign Affairs of the receiving State, or such other ministry as may be agreed, shall be notified of:
(a)   the appointment of members of the mission, their arrival and their final departure or the termination of their functions with the mission;
(b)   the arrival and final departure of a person belonging to the family of a member of the mission and, where appropriate, the fact that a person becomes or ceases to be a member of the family of a member of the mission;
(c)   the arrival and final departure of private servants in the employ of persons referred to in sub-paragraph (a) of this paragraph

and, where appropriate, the fact that they are leaving the employ of such persons;

(d)   the engagement and discharge of persons resident in the receiving State as members of the mission or private servants entitled to privileges and immunities.

2.   Where possible, prior notification of arrival and final departure shall also be given.

Article 11

1.   In the absence of specific agreement as to the size of the mission, the receiving State may require that the size of a mission be kept within limits considered by it to be reasonable and normal, having regard to circumstances and conditions in the receiving State and to the needs of the particular mission.

2.   The receiving State may equally, within similar bounds and on a non-discriminatory basis, refuse to accept officials of a particular category.

Article 12

The sending State may not, without the prior express consent of the receiving State, establish offices forming part of the mission in localities other than those in which the mission itself is established.

Article 13

1.   The head of the mission is considered as having taken up his functions in the receiving State either when he has presented his credentials of when he has notified his arrival and a true copy of his credentials has been presented to the Ministry for Foreign Affairs of the receiving State, or such other ministry as may be agreed, in accordance with the practice prevailing in the receiving State which shall be applied in a uniform manner.

2.   The order of presentation of credentials or of a true copy thereof will be determined by the date and time of the arrival of the head of the mission.

Article 14

1.   Heads of mission are divided into three classes, namely:

(a) that of ambassadors or nuncios accredited to Heads of State, and other heads of mission of equivalent rank;

(b) that of envoys, ministers and internuncios accredited to Heads of State;

(c) that of "chargés d'affaires" accredited to Ministers for Foreign Affairs.

2. Except as concerns precedence and etiquette, there shall be no differentiation between heads of mission by reason of their class.

Article 15

The class to which the heads of their missions are to be assigned shall be agreed between States.

Article 16

1. Heads of mission shall take precedence in their respective classes in the order of the date and time of taking up their functions in accordance with Article 13.

2. Alterations in the credentials of a head of mission not involving any change of class shall not affect his precedence.

3. This article is without prejudice to any practice accepted by the receiving State regarding the precedence of the representative of the Holy See.

Article 17

The precedence of the members of the diplomatic staff of the mission shall be notified by the head of the mission to the Ministry for Foreign Affairs or such other ministry as may be agreed.

Article 18

The procedure to be observed in each State for the reception of heads of mission shall be uniform in respect of each class.

Article 19

1. If the post of head of the mission is vacant, or if the head of the mission is unable to perform his functions, a "chargé d'affaires" *ad interim* shall act provisionally as head of the mission. The name of the "chargé d'affaires" ad interim shall be notified, either by the head of the mission or, in case he is unable to do

so, by the Ministry for Foreign Affairs of the sending State to the Ministry for Foreign Affairs of the receiving State or such other ministry as may be agreed.

2.   In cases where no member of the diplomatic staff of the mission is present in the receiving State, a member of the administrative and technical staff may, with the consent of the receiving State, be designated by the sending State to be in charge of the current administrative affairs of the mission.

Article 20

The mission and its head shall have the right to use the flag and emblem of the sending State on the premises of the mission, including the residence of the head of the mission, and on his means of transport.

Article 21

1.   The receiving State shall either facilitate the acquisition on its territory, in accordance with its laws, by the sending State of premises necessary for its mission or assist the latter in obtaining accommodation in some other way.
2.   It shall also, where necessary, assist missions in obtaining suitable accommodation for their members.

Article 22

1.   The premises of the mission shall be inviolable. The agents of the receiving State may not enter them, except with the consent of the head of the mission.
2.   The receiving State is under a special duty to take all appropriate steps to protect the premises of the mission against any intrusion or damage and to prevent any disturbance of the peace of the mission or impairment of its dignity.
3.   The premises of the mission, their furnishings and other property thereon and the means of transport of the mission shall be immune from search, requisition, attachment or execution.

Article 23

1.   The sending State and the head of the mission shall be exempt from all national, regional or municipal dues and taxes in respect

of the premises of the mission, whether owned or leased, other than such as represent payment for specific services rendered.

2. The exemption from taxation referred to in this Article shall not apply to such dues and taxes payable under the law of the receiving State by persons contracting with the sending State or the head of the mission.

Article 24

The archives and documents of the mission shall be inviolable at any time and wherever they may be.

Article 25

The receiving State shall accord full facilities for the performance of the functions of the mission.

Article 26

Subject to its laws and regulations concerning zones entry into which is prohibited or regulated for reasons of national security, the receiving State shall ensure to all members of the mission freedom of movement and travel in its territory.

Article 27

1. The receiving State shall permit and protect free communication on the part of the mission for all official purposes. In communicating with the Government and the other missions and consulates of the sending State, wherever situated, the mission may employ all appropriate means, including diplomatic couriers and messages in code or cipher. However, the mission may install and use a wireless transmitter only with the consent of the receiving State.
2. The official correspondence of the mission shall be inviolable. Official correspondence means all correspondence relating to the mission and its functions.
3. The diplomatic bag shall not be opened or detained.
4. The packages constituting the diplomatic bag must bear visible external marks of their character and may contain only diplomatic documents or articles intended for official use.

5. The diplomatic courier, who shall be provided with an official document indicating his status and the number of packages constituting the diplomatic bag, shall be protected by the receiving State in the performance of his functions. He shall enjoy personal inviolability and shall not be liable to any form of arrest or detention.
6. The sending State or the mission may designate diplomatic couriers ad hoc. In such cases the provisions of paragraph 5 of this Article shall also apply, except that the immunities therein mentioned shall cease to apply when such a courier has delivered to the consignee the diplomatic bag in his charge.
7. A diplomatic bag may be entrusted to the captain of a commercial aircraft scheduled to land at an authorized port of entry. He shall be provided with an official document indicating the number of packages constituting the bag but he shall not be considered to be a diplomatic courier. The mission may send one of its members to take possession of the diplomatic bag directly and freely from the captain of the aircraft.

Article 28
The fees and charges levied by the mission in the course of its official duties shall be exempt from all dues and taxes.

Article 29
The person of a diplomatic agent shall be inviolable. He shall not be liable to any form of arrest or detention. The receiving State shall treat him with due respect and shall take all appropriate steps to prevent any attack on his person, freedom or dignity.

Article 30
1. The private residence of a diplomatic agent shall enjoy the same inviolability and protection as the premises of the mission.
2. His papers, correspondence and, except as provided in paragraph 3 of Article 31, his property, shall likewise enjoy inviolability.

Article 31
1. A diplomatic agent shall enjoy immunity from the criminal jurisdiction of the receiving State. He shall also enjoy immunity from its civil and administrative jurisdiction, except in the case of:

(a)   a real action relating to private immovable property situated in the territory of the receiving State, unless he holds it on behalf of the sending State for the purposes of the mission;

(b)   an action relating to succession in which the diplomatic agent is involved as executor, administrator, heir or legatee as a private person and not on behalf of the sending State;

(c)   an action relating to any professional or commercial activity exercised by the diplomatic agent in the receiving State outside his official functions.

2.   A diplomatic agent is not obliged to give evidence as a witness.

3.   No measures of execution may be taken in respect of a diplomatic agent except in the cases coming under sub-paragraphs (a), (b) and (c) of paragraph 1 of this Article, and provided that the measures concerned can be taken without infringing the inviolability of his person or of his residence.

4.   The immunity of a diplomatic agent from the jurisdiction of the receiving State does not exempt him from the jurisdiction of the sending State.

Article 32

1.   The immunity from jurisdiction of diplomatic agents and of persons enjoying immunity under Article 37 may be waived by the sending State.

2.   Waiver must always be express.

3.   The initiation of proceedings by a diplomatic agent of by a person enjoying immunity from jurisdiction under Article 37 shall preclude him from invoking immunity from jurisdiction in respect of any counter-claim directly connected with the principal claim.

4.   Waiver of immunity from jurisdiction in respect of civil or administrative proceedings shall not be held to imply waiver of immunity in respect of the execution of the judgment, for which a separate waiver shall be necessary.

Article 33

1.   Subject to the provisions of paragraph 3 of this Article, a diplomatic agent shall with respect to services rendered for the sending State be exempt from social security provisions which may be in force in the receiving State.

2. The exemption provided for in paragraph 1 of this Article shall also apply to private servants who are in the sole employ of a diplomatic agent, on condition:

(a) that they are not nationals of or permanently resident in the receiving State, and

(b) that they are covered by the social security provisions which may be in force in the sending State or a third State.

3. A diplomatic agent who employs persons to whom the exemption provided for in paragraph 2 of this Article does not apply shall observe the obligations which the social security provision of the receiving State impose upon employers.

4. The exemption provided for in paragraphs 1 and 2 of this Article shall not preclude voluntary participation in the social security system of the receiving State provided that such participation is permitted by that State.

5. The provisions of this Article shall not affect bilateral or multilateral agreements concerning social security concluded previously and shall not prevent the conclusion of such agreements in the future.

Article 34

A diplomatic agent shall be exempt from all dues and taxes, personal or real, national, regional or municipal, except:

(a) indirect taxes of a kind which are normally incorporated in the price of goods or services;

(b) Dues and taxes on private immovable property situated in the territory of the receiving State, unless he holds it on behalf of the sending State for the purposes of the mission;

(c) estate, succession or inheritance duties levied by the receiving State, subject to the provisions of paragraph 4 of Article 39;

(d) dues and taxes on private income having its source in the receiving State and capital taxes on investments made in commercial undertakings in the receiving State;

(e) charges levied for specific services rendered;

(f) registration, court or record fees, mortgage dues and stamp duty, with respect to immovable property, subject to the provisions of Article 23.

Article 35

The receiving State shall exempt diplomatic agents from all personal services, from all public service of any kind whatsoever, and from military obligations such as those connected with requisitioning, military contributions and billeting.

Article 36

1. The receiving State shall, in accordance with such laws and regulations as it may adopt, permit entry of and grant exemption from all customs duties, taxes, and related charges other than charges for storage, cartage and similar services, on :

(a) articles for the official use of the mission;

(b) articles for their personal use of a diplomatic agent or members of his family forming part of his household, including articles intended for his establishment.

2. The personal baggage of a diplomatic agent shall be exempt from inspection, unless there are serious grounds for presuming that it contains articles not covered by the exemptions mentioned in paragraph 1 of this Article, or articles the import or export of which is prohibited by the law or controlled by the quarantine regulations of the receiving State. Such inspection shall be conducted only in the presence of the diplomatic agent or of his authorized representative.

Article 37

1. The members of the family of a diplomatic agent forming part of his household shall, if they are not nationals of the receiving State, enjoy the privileges and immunities specified in Articles 29 to 36.

2. Members of the administrative and technical staff of the mission, together with members of their families forming part of their respective households, shall, if they are not nationals of or permanently resident in the receiving State, enjoy the privileges and immunities specified in Articles 29 to 35, except that the immunity from civil and administrative jurisdiction of the receiving State specified in paragraph 1 of Article 31 shall not extend to acts performed outside the course of their duties. They shall also enjoy the privileges specified in Article 36, paragraph 1, in respect of articles imported at the time of first installation.

3.   Members of the service staff of the mission who are not nationals of or permanently resident in the receiving State shall enjoy immunity in respect of acts performed in the course of their duties, exemption from dues and taxes on the emoluments they receive by reason of their employment and the exemption contained in Article 33.

4.   Private servants of members of the mission shall, if they are not nationals of or permanently resident in the receiving State, be exempt from dues and taxes on the emoluments they receive by reason of their employment. In other respects, they may enjoy privileges and immunities only to the extent admitted by the receiving State. However, the receiving State must exercise its jurisdiction over those persons in such a manner as not to interfere unduly with the performance of the functions of the mission.

Article 38

1.   Except insofar as additional privileges and immunities may be granted by the receiving State, a diplomatic agent who is a national of or permanently resident in that State shall enjoy only immunity from jurisdiction, and inviolability, in respect of official acts performed in the exercise of his functions.

2.   Other members of the staff of the mission and private servants who are nationals of or permanently resident in the receiving State shall enjoy privileges and immunities only to the extent admitted by the receiving State. However, the receiving State must exercise its jurisdiction over those persons in such a manner as not to interfere unduly with the performance of the functions of the mission.

Article 39

1.   Every person entitled to privileges and immunities shall enjoy them from the moment he enters the territory of the receiving State on proceeding to take up his post or, if already in its territory, from the moment when his appointment is notified to the Ministry for Foreign Affairs or such other ministry as may be agreed.

2.   When the functions of a person enjoying privileges and immunities have come to an end, such privileges and immunities

shall normally cease at the moment when he leaves the country, or on expiry of a reasonable period in which to do so, but shall subsist until that time, even in case of armed conflict. However, with respect to acts performed by such a person in the exercise of his functions as a member of the mission, immunity shall continue to subsist.

3. In case of the death of a member of the mission, the members of his family shall continue to enjoy the privileges and immunities to which they are entitled until the expiry of a reasonable period in which to leave the country.

4. In the event of the death of a member of the mission not a national of or permanently resident in the receiving State or a member of his family forming part of his household, the receiving State shall permit the withdrawal of the movable property of the deceased, with the exception of any property acquired in the country the export of which was prohibited at the time of his death. Estate, succession and inheritance duties shall not be levied on movable property the presence of which in the receiving State was due solely to the presence there of the deceased as a member of the mission or as a member of the family of a member of the mission.

Article 40

1. If a diplomatic agent passes through or is in the territory of a third State, which has granted him a passport visa if such visa was necessary, while proceeding to take up or to return to his post, or when returning to his own country, the third State shall accord him inviolability and such other immunities as may be required to ensure his transit or return. The same shall apply in the case of any members of his family enjoying privileges and immunities who are accompanying the diplomatic agent, or traveling separately to join him or to return to their country.

2. In circumstances similar to those specified in paragraph 1 of this Article, third States shall not hinder the passage of members of the administrative and technical or service staff of a mission, and of members of their families, through their territories.

3. Third State shall accord to official correspondence and other official communications in transit, including messages in code

or cipher, the same freedom and protection as is accorded by the receiving State. They shall accord to diplomatic couriers, who have been granted a passport visa if such visa was necessary, and diplomatic bags in transit the same inviolability and protection as the receiving State is bound to accord.

4. The obligations of third States under paragraphs 1, 2 and 3 of this Article shall also apply to the persons mentioned respectively in those paragraphs, and to official communications and diplomatic bags, whose presence in the territory of the third State is due to force majeure

Article 41

1. Without prejudice to their privileges and immunities, it is the duty of all persons enjoying such privileges and immunities to respect the laws and regulations of the receiving State. They also have a duty not to interfere in the internal affairs of that State.
2. All official business with the receiving State entrusted to the mission by the sending State shall be conducted with or through the Ministry for Foreign Affairs of the receiving State or such other ministry as may be agreed.
3. The premises of the mission must not be used in any manner incompatible with the functions of the mission as laid down in the present Convention or by other rules of general international law or by any special agreements in force between the sending and the receiving State.

Article 42

A diplomatic agent shall not in the receiving State practise for personal profit any professional or commercial activity.

Article 43

The function of a diplomatic agent comes to an end, inter alia:
(a) on notification by the sending State to the receiving State that the function of the diplomatic agent has come to an end;
(b) on notification by the receiving State to the sending State that, in accordance with paragraph 2 of Article 9, it refuses to recognize the diplomatic agent as a member of the mission.

Article 44

The receiving State must, even in case of armed conflict, grant facilities in order to enable persons enjoying privileges and immunities, other than nationals of the receiving State, and members of the families of such persons irrespective of their nationality, to leave at the earliest possible moment. It must, in particular, in case of need, place at their disposal the necessary means of transport for themselves and their property.

Article 45

If diplomatic relations are broken off between two States, or if a mission is permanently or temporarily recalled:
(a)   the receiving State must, even in case of armed conflict, respect and protect the premises of the mission, together with its property and archives;
(b)   the sending State may entrust the custody of the premises of the mission, together with its property and archives, to a third State acceptable to the receiving State;
(c)   the sending State may entrust the protection of its interests and those of its nationals to a third State acceptable to the receiving State.

Article 46

A sending State may with the prior consent of a receiving State, and at the request of a third State not represented in the receiving State, undertake the temporary protection of the interests of the third State and of its nationals.

Article 47

1.   In the application of the provisions of the present Convention, the receiving State shall not discriminate as between States.
2.   However, discrimination shall not be regarded as taking place:
(a)   where the receiving State applies any of the provisions of the present Convention restrictively because of a restrictive application of that provision to its mission in the sending State;
(b)   where by custom or agreement States extend to each other more favourable treatment than is required by the provisions of the present Convention.

Article 48

The present Convention shall be open for signature by all States Members of the United Nations or of any of the specialized agencies or Parties to the Statute of the International Court of Justice, and by any other State invited by the General Assembly of the United Nations to become a Party to the Convention, as follows: until 31 October 1961 at the Federal Ministry for Foreign Affairs of Austria and subsequently, until 31 March 1962, at the United Nations Headquarters in New York.

Article 49

The present Convention is subject to ratification. The instruments of ratification shall be deposited with the Secretary-General of the United Nations.

Article 50

The present Convention shall remain open for accession by any State belonging to any of the four categories mentioned in Article 48. The instruments of accession shall be deposited with the Secretary-General of the United Nations.

Article 51

1. The present Convention shall enter into force on the thirtieth day following the date of deposit of the twenty-second instrument of ratification or accession with the Secretary-General of the United Nations.
2. For each State ratifying or acceding to the Convention after the deposit of the twenty-second instrument of ratification or accession, the Convention shall enter into force on the thirtieth day after deposit by such State of its instrument of ratification or accession.

Article 52

The Secretary-General of the United Nations shall inform all States belonging to any of the four categories mentioned in Article 48:

(a) of signatures to the present Convention and of the deposit of instruments of ratification or accession, in accordance with Articles 48, 49 and 50;

(b)   of the date on which the present Convention will enter into force, in accordance with Article 51.

Article 53

The original of the present Convention, of which the Chinese, English, French, Russian and Spanish texts are equally authentic, shall be deposited with the Secretary-General of the United Nations, who shall send certified copies thereof to all States belonging to any of the four categories mentioned in Article 48.

IN WITNESS WHEREOF the undersigned Plenipotentiaries, being duly authorized thereto by their respective Governments, have signed the present Convention.

DONE at Vienna, this eighteenth day of April one thousand nine hundred and sixty-one.

Annex
II

Vienna Convention on Consular Relations
Done at Vienna on 24 April 1963

The States Parties To The Present Convention,
RECALLING that consular relations have been established between peoples since ancient times,

HAVING IN MIND the Purposes and Principles of the Charter of the United Nations concerning the sovereign equality of States, the maintenance of international peace and security, and the promotion of friendly relations among nations,

CONSIDERING that the United Nations Conference on Diplomatic Intercourse and Immunities adopted the Vienna Convention on Diplomatic Relations, which was opened for signature on 18 April 1961,

BELIEVING that an international convention on consular relations, privileges and immunities would also contribute to the development of friendly relations among nations, irrespective of their differing constitutional and social systems,

REALIZING that the purpose of such privileges and immunities is not to benefit individuals but to ensure the efficient performance of functions by consular posts on behalf of their respective States,

AFFIRMING that the rules of customary international law continue to govern matters not expressly regulated by the provisions of the present Convention,

HAVE AGREED as follows:

Article 1
Definitions
1. For the purposes of the present Convention, the following expressions shall have the meanings hereunder assigned to them:
(a) "consular post" means any consulate-general, consulate, vice-consulate or consular agency;
(b) "consular district" means the area assigned to a consular post for the exercise of consular functions;
(c) "head of consular post" means the person charged with the duty of acting in that capacity;
(d) "consular officer" means any person, including the head of a consular post, entrusted in that capacity with the exercise of consular functions;
(e) "consular employee" means any person employed in the administrative or technical service of a consular post;
(f) "member of the service staff" means any person employed in the domestic service of a consular post;
(g) "members of the consular post" means consular officers, consular employees and members of the service staff;
(h) "members of the consular staff" means consular officers, other than the head of a consular post, consular employees and members of the service staff;
(i) "member of the private staff" means a person who is employed exclusively in the private service of a member of the consular post;
(j) "consular premises" means the buildings or parts of buildings and the land ancillary thereto, irrespective of ownership, used exclusively for the purposes of the consular post;
(k) "consular archives" includes all the papers, documents, correspondence, books, films, tapes and registers of the

consular post, together with the ciphers and codes, the card-indexes and any article of furniture intended for their protection or safekeeping.

2. Consular officers are of two categories, namely career consular officers and honorary consular officers. The provisions of Chapter II of the present Convention apply to consular posts headed by career consular officers; the provisions of Chapter III govern consular posts headed by honorary consular officers.

3. The particular status of members of the consular posts who are nationals or permanent residents of the receiving State is governed by Article 71 of the present Convention.

Chapter I - Consular Relations in General
Section I - Establishment and Conduct of Consular Relations

Article 2
Establishment of consular relations
1. The establishment of consular relations between States takes place by mutual consent.
2. The consent given to the establishment of diplomatic relations between two States implies, unless otherwise stated, consent to the establishment of consular relations.
3. The severance of diplomatic relations shall not *ipso facto* involve the severance of consular relations.

Article 3
Exercise of consular functions.
Consular functions are exercised by consular posts. They are also exercised by diplomatic missions in accordance with the provisions of the present Convention.

Article 4
Establishment of a consular post
1. A consular post may be established in the territory of the receiving State only with that State's consent.
2. The seat of the consular post, its classification and the consular district shall be established by the sending State and shall be subject to the approval of the receiving State.

3.   Subsequent changes in the seat of the consular post, its classification or the consular district may be made by the sending State only with the consent of the receiving State.
4.   The consent of the receiving State shall also be required if a consulate-general or a consulate desires to open a vice-consulate or a consular agency in a locality other than that in which it is itself established.
5.   The prior express consent of the receiving State shall also be required for the opening of an office forming part of an existing consular post elsewhere than at the seat thereof.

Article 5
Consular functions
Consular functions consist in:
(a)   protecting in the receiving State the interests of the sending State and of its nationals, both individuals and bodies corporate, within the limits permitted by international law;
(b)   furthering the development of commercial, economic, cultural and scientific relations between the sending State and the receiving State and otherwise promoting friendly relations between them in accordance with the provisions of the present Convention;
(c)   ascertaining by all lawful means conditions and developments in the commercial, economic, cultural and scientific life of the receiving State, reporting thereon to the Government of the sending State and giving information to persons interested;
(d)   issuing passports and travel documents to nationals of the sending State, and visas or appropriate documents to persons wishing to travel to the sending State;
(e)   helping and assisting nationals, both individuals and bodies corporate, of the sending State;
(f)   acting as notary and civil registrar and in capacities of a similar kind, and performing certain functions of an administrative nature, provided that there is nothing contrary thereto in the laws and regulations of the receiving State;
(g)   safeguarding the interests of nationals, both individuals and bodies corporate, of the sending State in cases of succession *mortis causa* in the territory of the receiving State, in accordance with the laws and regulations of the receiving State;

(h)   safeguarding, within the limits imposed by the laws and regulations of the receiving State, the interests of minors and other persons lacking full capacity who are nationals of the sending State, particularly where any guardianship or trusteeship is required with respect to such persons;

(i)   subject to the practices and procedures obtaining in the receiving State, representing or arranging appropriate representation for nationals of the sending State before the tribunals and other authorities of the receiving State, for the purpose of obtaining, in accordance with the laws and regulations of the receiving State, provisional measures for the preservation of the rights and interests of these nationals, where, because of absence or any other reason, such nationals are unable at the proper time to assume the defence of their rights and interests;

(j)   transmitting judicial and extra-judicial documents or executing letters rogatory or commissions to take evidence for the courts of the sending State in accordance with international agreements in force or, in the absence of such international agreements, in any other manner compatible with the laws and regulations of the receiving State;

(k)   exercising rights of supervision and inspection provided for in the laws and regulations of the sending State in respect of vessels having the nationality of the sending State, and of aircraft registered in that State, and in respect of their crews;

(l)   extending assistance to vessels and aircraft mentioned in sub-paragraph (k) of this Article and to their crews, taking statements regarding the voyage of a vessel, examining and stamping the ship's papers, and, without prejudice to the powers of the authorities of the receiving State, conducting investigations into any incidents which occurred during the voyage, and settling disputes of any kind between the master, the officers and the seamen in so far as this may be authorized by the laws and regulations of the sending State;

(m)   performing any other functions entrusted to a consular post by the sending State which are not prohibited by the laws and regulations of the receiving State or to which no objection is taken by the receiving State or which are referred to in the international agreements in force between the sending State and the receiving State.

Article 6

Exercise of consular functions outside the consular district
A consular officer may, in special circumstances, with the consent of the receiving State, exercise his functions outside his consular district.

Article 7

Exercise of consular functions in a third State
The sending State may, after notifying the States concerned, entrust a consular post established in a particular State with the exercise of consular functions in another State, unless there is express objection by one of the States concerned.

Article 8

Exercise of consular functions on behalf of a third State
Upon appropriate notification to the receiving State, a consular post of the sending State may, unless the receiving State objects, exercise consular functions in the receiving State on behalf of a third State.

Article 9

Classes of heads of consular posts
1. Heads of consular posts are divided into four classes, namely:
(a) consuls-general;
(b) consuls;
(c) vice-consuls;
(d) consular agents.
2. Paragraph 1 of this Article in no way restricts the right of any of the Contracting Parties to fix the designation of consular officers other than the heads of consular posts.

Article 10

Appointment and admission of heads of consular posts
1. Heads of consular posts are appointed by the sending State and are admitted to the exercise of their functions by the receiving State.
2. Subject to the provisions of the present Convention, the formalities for the appointment and for the admission of the head of a consular post are determined by the laws, regulations and usages of the sending State and of the receiving State respectively.

Article 11

The consular commission or notification of appointment

1. The head of a consular post shall be provided by the sending State with a document, in the form of a commission or similar instrument, made out for each appointment, certifying his capacity and showing, as a general rule, his full name, his category and class, the consular district and the seat of the consular post.
2. The sending State shall transmit the commission or similar instrument through the diplomatic or other appropriate channel to the government of the State in whose territory the head of a consular post is to exercise his functions.
3. If the receiving State agrees, the sending State may, instead of a commission or similar instrument, send to the receiving State a notification containing the particulars required by paragraph 1 of this Article.

Article 12

The exequatur

1. The head of a consular post is admitted to the exercise of his functions by an authorization from the receiving State termed an *exequatur*, whatever the form of this authorization.
2. A State which refuses to grant an *exequatur* is not obliged to give to the sending State reasons for such refusal.
3. Subject to the provisions of Articles 13 and 15, the head of a consular post shall not enter upon his duties until he has received an *exequatur*.

Article 13

Provisional admission of heads of consular posts

Pending delivery of the *exequatur*, the head of a consular post may be admitted on a provisional basis to the exercise of his functions. In that case, the provisions of the present Convention shall apply.

Article 14

Notification to the authorities of the consular district.

As soon as the head of a consular post is admitted even provisionally to the exercise of his functions, the receiving State shall immediately notify the competent authorities of the consular district. It shall also ensure that the necessary measures are taken to enable the head of a consular post to carry out the duties of his office and to have the benefit of the provisions of the present Convention.

Article 15

Temporary exercise of the functions of the head of a consular post

1. If the head of a consular post is unable to carry out his functions or the position of head of consular post is vacant, an acting head of post may act provisionally as head of the consular post.
2. The full name of the acting head of post shall be notified either by the diplomatic mission of the sending State or, if that State has no such mission in the receiving State, by the head of the consular post, or, if he is unable to do so, by any competent authority of the sending State, to the Ministry for Foreign Affairs of the receiving State or to the authority designated by that Ministry. As a general rule, this notification shall be given in advance. The receiving State may make the admission as acting head of post of a person who is neither a diplomatic agent nor a consular officer of the sending State in the receiving State conditional on its consent.
3. The competent authorities of the receiving State shall afford assistance and protection to the acting head of post. While he is in charge of the post, the provisions of the present Convention shall apply to him on the same basis as to the head of the consular post concerned. The receiving State shall not, however, be obliged to grant to an acting head of post any facility, privilege or immunity which the head of the consular post enjoys only subject to conditions not fulfilled by the acting head of post.
4. When, in the circumstances referred to in paragraph 1 of this Article, a member of the diplomatic staff of the diplomatic mission of the sending State in the receiving State is designated by the sending State as an acting head of post, he shall, if the receiving State does not object thereto, continue to enjoy diplomatic privileges and immunities.

Article 16

Precedence as between heads of consular posts

1. Heads of consular posts shall rank in each class according to the date of the grant of the *exequatur*.

2. If, however, the head of a consular post before obtaining the *exequatur* is admitted to the exercise of his functions provisionally, his precedence shall be determined according to the date of the provisional admission; this precedence shall be maintained after the granting of the *exequatur*.

3. The order of precedence as between two or more heads of consular posts who obtained the *exequatur* or provisional admission on the same date shall be determined according to the dates on which their commissions or similar instruments or the notifications referred to in paragraph 3 of Article 11 were presented to the receiving State.

4. Acting heads of posts shall rank after all heads of consular posts and, as between themselves, they shall rank according to the dates on which they assumed their functions as acting heads of posts as indicated in the notifications given under paragraph 2 of Article 15.

5. Honorary consular officers who are heads of consular posts shall rank in each class after career heads of consular posts, in the order and according to the rules laid down in the foregoing paragraphs.

6. Heads of consular posts shall have precedence over consular officers not having that status.

Article 17

Performance of diplomatic acts by consular officers

1. In a State where the sending State has no diplomatic mission and is not represented by a diplomatic mission of a third State, a consular officer may, with the consent of the receiving State, and without affecting his consular status, be authorised to perform diplomatic acts. The performance of such acts by a consular officer shall not confer upon him any right to claim diplomatic privileges and immunities.

2. A consular officer may, after notification addressed to the receiving State, act as representative of the sending State to any inter-governmental organisation. When so acting, he shall be entitled to enjoy any privileges and immunities accorded to such a representative by customary international law or by international agreements; however, in respect of the performance by him of

any consular function, he shall not be entitled to any greater immunity from jurisdiction than that to which a consular officer is entitled under the present Convention.

Article 18

Appointment of the same person by two or more States as a consular officer. Two or more States may, with the consent of the receiving State, appoint the same person as a consular officer in that State.

Article 19

Appointment of members of consular staff
1. Subject to the provisions of Articles 20, 22 and 23, the sending State may freely appoint the members of the consular staff.
2. The full name, category and class of all consular officers, other than the head of a consular post, shall be notified by the sending State to the receiving State in sufficient time for the receiving State, if it so wishes, to exercise its rights under paragraph 3 of Article 23.
3. The sending State may, if required by its laws and regulations, request the receiving State to grant an *exequatur* to a consular officer other than the head of a consular post.
4. The receiving State may, if required by its laws and regulations, grant an *exequatur* to a consular officer other than the head of a consular post.

Article 20

Size of the consular staff. In the absence of an express agreement as to the size of the consular staff, the receiving State may require that the size of the staff be kept within limits considered by it to be reasonable and normal, having regard to circumstances and conditions in the consular district and to the needs of the particular consular post.

Article 21

Precedence as between consular officers of a consular post. The order of precedence as between the consular officers of a consular post and any change thereof shall be notified by the diplomatic mission of the sending State or, if that State has no such mission in the receiving State, by the head of the consular post, to the Ministry for Foreign

Affairs of the receiving State or to the authority designated by that Ministry.

Article 22

Nationality of consular officers.
1. Consular officers should, in principle, have the nationality of the sending State.
2. Consular officers may not be appointed from among persons having the nationality of the receiving State except with the express consent of that State which may be withdrawn at any time.
3. The receiving State may reserve the same right with regard to nationals of a third State who are not also nationals of the sending State.

Article 23

Persons declared non grata
1. The receiving State may at any time notify the sending State that a consular officer is *persona non grata* or that any other member of the consular staff is not acceptable. In that event, the sending State shall, as the case may be, either recall the person concerned or terminate his functions with the consular post.
2. If the sending State refuses or fails within a reasonable time to carry out its obligations under paragraph 1 of this Article, the receiving State may, as the case may be, either withdraw the *exequatur* from the person concerned or cease to consider him as a member of the consular staff.
3. A person appointed as a member of a consular post may be declared unacceptable before arriving in the territory of the receiving State or, if already in the receiving State, before entering on his duties with the consular post. In any such case, the sending State shall withdraw his appointment.
4. In the cases mentioned in paragraphs 1 and 3 of this Article, the receiving State is not obliged to give to the sending State reasons for its decision.

Article 24

Notification to the receiving State of appointments, arrivals and departures.

1. The Ministry for Foreign Affairs of the receiving State or the authority designated by that Ministry shall be notified of:

(a) the appointment of members of a consular post, their arrival after appointment to the consular post, their final departure or the termination of their functions and any other changes affecting their status that may occur in the course of their service with the consular post;

(b) the arrival and final departure of a person belonging to the family of a member of a consular post forming part of his household and, where appropriate, the fact that a person becomes or ceases to be such a member of the family;

(c) the arrival and final departure of members of the private staff and, where appropriate, the termination of their service as such;

(d) the engagement and discharge of persons resident in the receiving State as members of a consular post or as members of the private staff entitled to privileges and immunities.

2. When possible, prior notification of arrival and final departure shall also be given.

Section II. End of Consular functions
Article 25

Termination of the functions of a member of a consular post
The functions of a member of a consular post shall come to an end *inter alia*:

(a) on notification by the sending State to the receiving State that his functions have come to an end;

(b) on withdrawal of the *exequatur*;

(c) on notification by the receiving State to the sending State that the receiving State has ceased to consider him as a member of the consular staff.

Article 26

Departure from the territory of the receiving State. The receiving State shall, even in case of armed conflict, grant to members of the consular post and members of the private staff, other than nationals of the receiving State, and to members of their families forming part of their households irrespective of nationality, the necessary time and facilities to enable them to prepare their departure and to leave at the earliest possible moment after the termination of the functions of the members concerned. In particular, it shall, in case of need, place at their disposal the necessary means of transport for themselves and their property other than property acquired in the receiving State the export of which is prohibited at the time of departure.

Article 27

Protection of consular premises and archives and of the interests of the sending State in exceptional circumstances

1. In the event of the severance of consular relations between two States:
(a) the receiving State shall, even in case of armed conflict, respect and protect the consular premises, together with the property of the consular post and the consular archives,
(b) the sending State may entrust the custody of the consular premises, together with the property contained therein and the consular archives, to a third State acceptable to the receiving State;
(c) the sending State may entrust the protection of its interests and those of its nationals to a third State acceptable to the receiving State.
2. In the event of the temporary or permanent closure of a consular post, the provisions of sub-paragraph (a) of paragraph 1 of this Article shall apply. In addition,
(a) if the sending State, although not represented in the receiving State by a diplomatic mission, has another consular post in the territory of that State, that consular post may be entrusted with the custody of the premises of the consular post which has been closed, together with the property contained therein and the consular archives, and, with the consent of the receiving State, with the exercise of consular functions in the district of that consular post; or
(b) if the sending State has no diplomatic mission and no other consular post in the receiving State, the provisions of sub-paragraphs (b) and (c) of paragraph 1 of this Article shall apply.

Chapter I. Facilities, Privileges And Immunities Relating to Consular Posts, Career Consular Officers and other Members of A Consular Post

Section 1. Facilities, Privileges and Immunities Relating to a Consular Post

Article 28
Facilities for the work of the consular post . The receiving State shall accord full facilities for the performance of the functions of the consular post.

Article 29
Use of national flag and coat-of-arms
1.   The sending State shall have the right to the use of its national flag and coat-of-arms in the receiving State in accordance with the provisions of this Article.
2.   The national flag of the sending State may be flown and its coat-of-arms displayed on the building occupied by the consular post and at the entrance door thereof, on the residence of the head of the consular post and on his means of transport when used on official business.
3.   In the exercise of the right accorded by this Article regard shall be had to the laws, regulations and usages of the receiving State.

Article 30
Accommodation
1.   The receiving State shall either facilitate the acquisition on its territory, in accordance with its laws and regulations, by the sending State of premises necessary for its consular post or assist the latter in obtaining accommodation in some other way.
2.   It shall also, where necessary, assist the consular post in obtaining suitable accommodation for its members.

Article 31
Inviolability of the consular premises
1.   Consular premises shall be inviolable to the extent provided in this Article.

2. The authorities of the receiving State shall not enter that part of the consular premises which is used exclusively for the purpose of the work of the consular post except with the consent of the head of the consular post or of his designee or of the head of the diplomatic mission of the sending State. The consent of the head of the consular post may, however, be assumed in case of fire or other disaster requiring prompt protective action.
3. Subject to the provisions of paragraph 2 of this Article, the receiving State is under a special duty to take all appropriate steps to protect the consular premises against any intrusion or damage and to prevent any disturbance of the peace of the consular post or impairment of its dignity.
4. The consular premises, their furnishings, the property of the consular post and its means of transport shall be immune from any form of requisition for purposes of national defence or public utility. If expropriation is necessary for such purposes, all possible steps shall be taken to avoid impeding the performance of consular functions, and prompt, adequate and effective compensation shall be paid to the sending State.

Article 32
Exemption from taxation of consular premises
1. Consular premises and the residence of the career head of consular post of which the sending State or any person acting on its behalf is the owner or lessee shall be exempt from all national, regional or municipal dues and taxes whatsoever, other than such as represent payment for specific services rendered.
2. The exemption from taxation referred to in paragraph 1 of this Article shall not apply to such dues and taxes if; under the law of the receiving State, they are payable by the person who contracted with the sending State or with the person acting on its behalf.

Article 33
Inviolability of the consular archives and documents
The consular archives and documents shall be inviolable at all times and wherever they may be.

Article 34
Freedom of movement
Subject to its laws and regulations concerning zones entry into which is prohibited or regulated for reasons of national security, the receiving State shall ensure freedom of movement and travel in its territory to all members of the consular post.

Article 35
Freedom of communication
1. The receiving State shall permit and protect freedom of communication on the part of the consular post for all official purposes. In communicating with the Government, the diplomatic missions and other consular posts, wherever situated, of the sending State, the consular post may employ all appropriate means, including diplomatic or consular couriers, diplomatic or consular bags and messages in code or cipher. However, the consular post may install and use a wireless transmitter only with the consent of the receiving State.
2. The official correspondence of the consular post shall be inviolable. Official correspondence means all correspondence relating to the consular post and its functions.
3. The consular bag shall be neither opened nor detained. Nevertheless, if the competent authorities of the receiving State have serious reason to believe that the bag contains something other than the correspondence, documents or articles referred to in paragraph 4 of this Article, they may request that the bag be opened in their presence by an authorised representative of the sending State. If this request is refused by the authorities of the sending State, the bag shall be returned to its place of origin.
4. The packages constituting the consular bag shall bear visible external marks of their character and may contain only official correspondence and documents or articles intended exclusively for official use.
5. The consular courier shall be provided with an official document indicating his status and the number of packages constituting the consular bag. Except with the consent of the receiving State he shall be neither a national of the receiving State, nor, unless he is a national of the sending State, a permanent resident of the

receiving State. In the performance of his functions he shall be protected by the receiving State. He shall enjoy personal inviolability and shall not be liable to any form of arrest or detention.

6. The sending State, its diplomatic missions and its consular posts may designate consular couriers *ad hoc*. In such cases the provisions of paragraph 5 of this Article shall also apply except that the immunities therein mentioned shall cease to apply when such a courier has delivered to the consignee the consular bag in his charge.

7. A consular bag may be entrusted to the captain of a ship or of a commercial aircraft scheduled to land at an authorized port of entry. He shall be provided with an official document indicating the number of packages constituting the bag, but he shall not be considered to be a consular courier. By arrangement with the appropriate local authorities, the consular post may send one of its members to take possession of the bag directly and freely from the captain of the ship or of the aircraft.

Article 36
Communication and contact with nationals of the sending State

1. With a view to facilitating the exercise of consular functions relating to nationals of the sending State:

(a) consular officers shall be free to communicate with nationals of the sending State and to have access to them. Nationals of the sending State shall have the same freedom with respect to communication with and access to consular officers of the sending State;

(b) if he so requests, the competent authorities of the receiving State shall, without delay, inform the consular post of the sending State if, within its consular district, a national of that State is arrested or committed to prison or to custody pending trial or is detained in any other manner. Any communication addressed to the consular post by the person arrested, in prison, custody or detention shall also be forwarded by the said authorities without delay. The said authorities shall inform the person concerned without delay of his rights under this sub-paragraph;

(c)   consular officers shall have the right to visit a national of the sending State who is in prison, custody or detention, to converse and correspond with him and to arrange for his legal representation. They shall also have the right to visit any national of the sending State who is in prison, custody or detention in their district in pursuance of a judgment. Nevertheless, consular officers shall refrain from taking action on behalf of a national who is in prison, custody or detention if he expressly opposes such action.

2.   The rights referred to in paragraph 1 of this Article shall be exercised in conformity with the laws and regulations of the receiving State, subject to the proviso, however, that the said laws and regulations must enable full effect to be given to the purposes for which the rights accorded under this Article are intended.

Article 37
Information in cases of deaths, guardianship or trusteeship, wrecks and air accidents
If the relevant information is available to the competent authorities of the receiving State, such authorities shall have the duty:

(a)   in the case of the death of a national of the sending State, to inform without delay the consular post in whose district the death occurred;

b)   to inform the competent consular post without delay of any case where the appointment of a guardian or trustee appears to be in the interests of a minor or other person lacking full capacity who is a national of the sending State. The giving of this information shall, however, be without prejudice to the operation of the laws and regulations of the receiving State concerning such appointments;

(c)   if a vessel, having the nationality of the sending State, is wrecked or runs aground in the territorial sea or internal waters of the receiving State, or if an aircraft registered in the sending State suffers an accident on the territory of the receiving State, to inform without delay the consular post nearest to the scene of the occurrence.

Article 38

Communication with the authorities of the receiving State
In the exercise of their functions, consular officers may address:
(a) the competent local authorities of their consular district;
(b) the competent central authorities of the receiving State if and to the extent that this is allowed by the laws, regulations and usages of the receiving State or by the relevant international agreements.

Article 39

Consular fees and charges
1. The consular post may levy in the territory of the receiving State the fees and charges provided by the laws and regulations of the sending State for consular acts.
2. The sums collected in the form of the fees and charges referred to in paragraph 1 of this Article, and the receipts for such fees and charges, shall be exempt from all dues and taxes in the receiving State.

Section I. Facilities, Privileges And Immunities Relating to Career Consular Officers and other Members of a Consular Post

Article 40

Protection of consular officers. The receiving State shall treat consular officers with due respect and shall take all appropriate steps to prevent any attack on their person, freedom or dignity.

Article 41

Personal inviolability of consular officers
1. Consular officers shall not be liable to arrest or detention pending trial, except in the case of a grave crime and pursuant to a decision by the competent judicial authority.
2. Except in the case specified in paragraph 1 of this Article, consular officers shall not be committed to prison or liable to any other form of restriction on their personal freedom save in execution of a judicial decision of final effect.
3. If criminal proceedings are instituted against a consular officer, he must appear before the competent authorities. Nevertheless, the proceedings shall be conducted with the respect due to him

by reason of his official position and, except in the case specified in paragraph 1 of this Article, in a manner which will hamper the exercise of consular functions as little as possible. When, in the circumstances mentioned in paragraph 1 of this Article, it has become necessary to detain a consular officer, the proceedings against him shall be instituted with the minimum of delay.

Article 42

Notification of arrest, detention or prosecution.

In the event of the arrest or detention, pending trial, of a member of the consular staff, or of criminal proceedings being instituted against him, the receiving State shall promptly notify the head of the consular post. Should the latter be himself the object of any such measure, the receiving State shall notify the sending State through the diplomatic channel.

Article 43

Immunity from jurisdiction

1.   Consular officers and consular employees shall not be amenable to the jurisdiction of the judicial or administrative authorities of the receiving State in respect of acts performed in the exercise of consular functions.
2.   The provisions of paragraph 1 of this Article shall not, however, apply in respect of a civil action either:
(a)   arising out of a contract concluded by a consular officer or a consular employee in which he did not contract expressly or impliedly as an agent of the sending State; or
(b)   by a third party for damage arising from an accident in the receiving State caused by a vehicle, vessel or aircraft.

Article 44

Liability to give evidence

1.   Members of a consular post may be called upon to attend as witnesses in the course of judicial or administrative proceedings. A consular employee or a member of the service staff shall not, except in the cases mentioned in paragraph 3 of this Article, decline to give evidence. If a consular officer should decline to do so, no coercive measure or penalty may be applied to him.

2. The authority requiring the evidence of a consular officer shall avoid interference with the performance of his functions. It may, when possible, take such evidence at his residence or at the consular post or accept a statement from him in writing.
3. Members of a consular post are under no obligation to give evidence concerning matters connected with the exercise of their functions or to produce official correspondence and documents relating thereto. They are also entitled to decline to give evidence as expert witnesses with regard to the law of the sending State.

Article 45
Waiver of privileges and immunities
1. The sending State may waive, with regard to a member of the consular post, any of the privileges and immunities provided for in Articles 41, 43 and 44.
2. The waiver shall in all cases be express, except as provided in paragraph 3 of this Article, and shall be communicated to the receiving State in writing.
3. The initiation of proceedings by a consular officer or a consular employee in a matter where he might enjoy immunity from jurisdiction under Article 43 shall preclude him from invoking immunity from jurisdiction in respect of any counter-claim directly connected with the principal claim.
4. The waiver of immunity from jurisdiction for the purposes of civil or administrative proceedings shall not be deemed to imply the waiver of immunity from the measures of execution resulting from the judicial decision; in respect of such measures, a separate waiver shall be necessary.

Article 46
Exemption from registration of aliens and residence permits
1. Consular officers and consular employees and members of their families forming part of their households shall be exempt from all obligations under the laws and regulations of the receiving State in regard to the registration of aliens and residence permits.
2. The provisions of paragraph 1 of this Article shall not, however, apply to any consular employee who is not a permanent employee of the sending State or who carries on any private gainful

occupation in the receiving State or to any member of the family of any such employee.

Article 47
Exemption from work permits

1. Members of the consular post shall, with respect to services rendered for the sending State, be exempt from any obligations in regard to work permits imposed by the laws and regulations of the receiving State concerning the employment of foreign labour.

2. Members of the private staff of consular officers and of consular employees shall, if they do not carry on any other gainful occupation in the receiving State, be exempt from the obligations referred to in paragraph 1 of this Article.

Article 48
Social security exemption

1. Subject to the provisions of paragraph 3 of this Article, members of the consular post with respect to services rendered by them for the sending State, and members of their families forming part of their households, shall be exempt from social security provisions which may be in force in the receiving State.

2. The exemption provided for in paragraph 1 of this Article shall apply also to members of the private staff who are in the sole employ of members of the consular post, on condition;

(a) that they are not nationals of or permanently resident in the receiving State; and

(b) that they are covered by the social security provisions which are in force in the sending State or a third State.

3. Members of the consular post who employ persons to whom the exemption provided for in paragraph 2 of this Article does not apply shall observe the obligations which the social security provisions of the receiving State impose upon employers.

4. The exemption provided for in paragraphs 1 and 2 of this Article shall not preclude voluntary participation in the social security system of the receiving State, provided that such participation is permitted by that State.

Article 49

Exemption from taxation.

1. Consular officers and consular employees and members of their families forming part of their households shall be exempt from all dues and taxes, personal or real, national, regional or municipal, except:

(a) indirect taxes of a kind which are normally incorporated in the price of goods or services;

(b) dues or taxes on private immovable property situated in the territory of the receiving State, subject to the provisions of Article 32;

(c) estate, succession or inheritance duties on transfers, levied by the receiving State, subject to the provisions of paragraph (b) of Article 51;

(d) dues and taxes on private income, including capital gains, having its source in the receiving State and capital taxes relating to investments made in commercial or financial undertakings in the receiving State;

(e) charges levied for specific services rendered;

(f) registration, court or record fees, mortgage dues and stamp duties, subject to the provisions of Article 32.

2. Members of the service staff shall be exempt from dues and taxes on the wages which they receive for their services.

3. Members of the consular post who employ persons whose wages or salaries are not exempt from income tax in the receiving State shall observe the obligations which the laws and regulations of that State impose upon employers concerning the levying of income tax.

Article 50

Exemption from customs duties and inspection

1. The receiving State shall, in accordance with such laws and regulations as it may adopt, permit entry of and grant exemption from all customs duties, taxes, and related charges other than charges for storage, cartage and similar services, on:

(a) articles for the official use of the consular post;

(b) articles for the personal use of a consular officer or members of his family forming part of his household, including articles intended for his establishment. The articles intended for consumption shall not exceed the quantities necessary for direct utilisation by the persons concerned.

2. Consular employees shall enjoy the privileges and exemptions specified in paragraph 1 of this article in respect of articles imported at the time of first installation.

3. Personal baggage accompanying consular officers and members of their families forming part of their households shall be exempt from inspection. It may be inspected only if there is serious reason to believe that it contains articles other than those referred to in sub-paragraph (b) of paragraph 1 of this Article, or articles the import or export of which is prohibited by the laws and regulations of the receiving State or which are subject to its quarantine laws and regulations. Such inspection shall be carried out in the presence of the consular officer or member of his family concerned.

Article 51

Estate of a member of the consular post or of a member of his family In the event of the death of a member of the consular post or of a member of his family forming part of his household, the receiving State:

(a) hall permit the export of the movable property of the deceased, with the exception of any such property acquired in the receiving State the export of which was prohibited at the time of his death;

(b) shall not levy national, regional or municipal estate, succession or inheritance duties, and duties on transfers, on movable property the presence of which in the receiving State was due solely to the presence in that State of the deceased as a member of the consular post or as a member of the family of a member of the consular post.

Article 52

Exemption from personal services and contributions. The receiving State shall exempt members of the consular post and members of their families forming part of their households from all personal services, from all public service of any kind whatsoever, and from military obligations such as those connected with requisitioning, military contributions and billeting.

Article 53
Beginning and end of consular privileges and immunities
1. Every member of the consular post shall enjoy the privileges and immunities provided in the present Convention from the moment he enters the territory of the receiving State on proceeding to take up his post or, if already in its territory, from the moment when he enters on his duties with the consular post.
2. Members of the family of a member of the consular post forming part of his household and members of his private staff shall receive the privileges and immunities provided in the present Convention from the date from which he enjoys privileges and immunities in accordance with paragraph 1 of this Article or from the date of their entry into the territory of the receiving State or from the date of their becoming a member of such family or private staff, whichever is the latest.
3. When the functions of a member of the consular post have come to an end, his privileges and immunities and those of a member of his family forming part of his household or a member of his private staff shall normally cease at the moment when the person concerned leaves the receiving State or on the expiry of a reasonable period in which to do so, whichever is the sooner, but shall subsist until that time, even in case of armed conflict. In the case of the persons referred to in paragraph 2 of this Article, their privileges and immunities shall come to an end when they cease to belong to the household or to be in the service of a member of the consular post provided, however, that if such persons intend leaving the receiving State within a reasonable period thereafter, their privileges and immunities shall subsist until the time of their departure.
4. However, with respect to acts performed by a consular officer or a consular employee in the exercise of his functions, immunity from jurisdiction shall continue to subsist without limitation of time.
5. In the event of the death of a member of the consular post, the members of his family forming part of his household shall continue to enjoy the privileges and immunities accorded to them until they leave the receiving State or until the expiry of a reasonable period enabling them to do so, whichever is the sooner.

Article 54
Obligations of third States
1. If a consular officer passes through or is in the territory of a third State, which has granted him a visa if a visa was necessary, while proceeding to take up or return to his post or when returning to the sending State, the third State shall accord to him all immunities provided for by the other Articles of the present Convention as may be required to ensure his transit or return. The same shall apply in the case of any member of his family forming part of his household enjoying such privileges and immunities who are accompanying the consular officer or travelling separately to join him or to return to the sending State.
2. In circumstances similar to those specified in paragraph 1 of this Article, third States shall not hinder the transit through their territory of other members of the consular post or of members of their families forming part of their households.
3. Third States shall accord to official correspondence and to other official communications in transit, including messages in code or cipher, the same freedom and protection as the receiving State is bound to accord under the present Convention. They shall accord to consular couriers who have been granted a visa, if a visa was necessary, and to consular bags in transit, the same inviolability and protection as the receiving State is bound to accord under the present Convention.
4. The obligations of third States under paragraphs 1, 2 and 3 of this Article shall also apply to the persons mentioned respectively in those paragraphs, and to official communications and to consular bags, whose presence in the territory of the third State is due to *force majeure*.

Article 55
Respect for the laws and regulations of the receiving State
1. Without prejudice to their privileges and immunities, it is the duty of all persons enjoying such privileges and immunities to respect the laws and regulations of the receiving State. They also have a duty not to interfere in the internal affairs of that State.
2. The consular premises shall not be used in any manner incompatible with the exercise of consular functions.

3.   The provisions of paragraph 2 of this Article shall not exclude the possibility of offices of other institutions or agencies being installed in part of the building in which the consular premises are situated, provided that the premises assigned to them are separate from those used by the consular post. In that event, the said offices shall not, for the purposes of the present Convention, be considered to form part of the consular premises.

Article 56

Insurance against third party risks. Members of the consular post shall comply with any requirement imposed by the laws and regulations of the receiving State in respect of insurance against third party risks arising from the use of any vehicle, vessel or aircraft.

Article 57

Special provisions concerning private gainful occupation
1.   Career consular officers shall not carry on for personal profit any professional or commercial activity in the receiving State.
2.   Privileges and immunities provided in this Chapter shall not be accorded:
(a)   to consular employees or to members of the service staff who carry on any private gainful occupation in the receiving State;
(b)   to members of the family of a person referred to in sub-paragraph

(a)   of this paragraph or to members of his private staff;
(c)   to members of the family of a member of a consular post who themselves carry on any private gainful occupation in the receiving State.

Chapter III. Regime Relating to Honorary Consular Officers And Consular Posts Headed by Such Officers

Article 58

General provisions relating to facilities, privileges and immunities
1.   Articles 28, 29, 30, 34, 35, 36, 37, 38 and 39, paragraph 3 of Article 54 and paragraphs 2 and 3 of Article 55 shall apply to consular posts headed by an honorary consular officer. In

addition, the facilities, privileges and immunities of such consular posts shall be governed by Articles 59, 60, 61 and 62.

2. Articles 42 and 43, paragraph 3 of Article 44, Articles 45 and 53 and paragraph 1 of Article 55 shall apply to honorary consular officers. In addition, the facilities, privileges and immunities of such consular officers shall be governed by Articles 63, 64, 65, 66 and 67.

3. Privileges and immunities provided in the present Convention shall not be accorded to members of the family of an honorary consular officer or of a consular employee employed at a consular post headed by an honorary consular officer.

4. The exchange of consular bags between two consular posts headed by honorary consular officers in different States shall not be allowed without the consent of the two receiving States concerned.

Article 59

Protection of the consular premises. The receiving State shall take steps as may be necessary to protect the consular premises of a consular post headed by an honorary consular officer against any intrusion or damage and to prevent any disturbance of the peace of the consular post or impairment of its dignity.

Article 60

Exemption from taxation of consular premises

1. Consular premises of a consular post headed by an honorary consular officer of which the sending State is the owner or lessee shall be exempt from all national, regional or municipal dues and taxes whatsoever, other than such as represent payment for specific services rendered.

2. The exemption from taxation referred to in paragraph 1 of this Article shall not apply to such dues and taxes if, under the laws and regulations of the receiving State, they are payable by the person who contracted with the sending State.

Article 61

Inviolability of consular archives and documents. The consular archives and documents of a consular post headed by an honorary consular officer shall be inviolable at all times and wherever they may be, provided that they are kept separate from other papers and documents and, in particular, from the private correspondence of the head of a consular post and of any person working with him, and from the materials, books or documents relating to their profession or trade.

Article 62
Exemption from customs duties. The receiving State shall, in accordance with such laws and regulations as it may adopt, permit entry of, and grant exemption from all customs duties, taxes, and related charges other than charges for storage, cartage and similar services on the following articles, provided that they are for the official use of a consular post headed by an honorary consular officer: coats-of-arms, flags, signboards, seals and stamps, books, official printed matter, office furniture, office equipment and similar articles supplied by or at the instance of the sending State to the consular post.

Article 63
Criminal proceedings. If criminal proceedings are instituted against an honorary consular officer, he must appear before the competent authorities. Nevertheless, the proceedings shall be conducted with the respect due to him by reason of his official position and, except when he is under arrest or detention, in a manner which will hamper the exercise of consular functions as little as possible. When it has become necessary to detain an honorary consular officer, the proceedings against him shall be instituted with the minimum of delay.

Article 64
Protection of honorary consular officers. The receiving State is under a duty to accord to an honorary consular officer such protection as may be required by reason of his official position.

Article 65
Exemption from registration of aliens and residence permits. Honorary consular officers, with the exception of those who carry on for personal profit any professional or commercial activity in the receiving State, shall be exempt from all obligations under the laws and regulations of the receiving State in regard to the registration of aliens and residence permits.

Article 66

Exemption from taxation. An honorary consular officer shall be exempt from all dues and taxes on the remuneration and emoluments which he receives from the sending State in respect of the exercise of consular functions.

Article 67

Exemption from personal services and contributions. The receiving State shall exempt honorary consular officers from all personal services and from all public services of any kind whatsoever and from military obligations such as those connected with requisitioning, military contributions and billeting.

Article 68

Optional character of the institution of honorary consular officers. Each State is free to decide whether it will appoint or receive honorary consular officers.

Chapter IV   General Provisions
Article 69

Consular agents who are not heads of consular posts
1. Each State is free to decide whether it will establish or admit consular agencies conducted by consular agents not designated as heads of consular post by the sending State.
2. The conditions under which the consular agencies referred to in paragraph 1 of this Article may carry on their activities and the privileges and immunities which may be enjoyed by the consular agents in charge of them shall be determined by agreement between the sending State and the receiving State.

Article 70

Exercise of consular functions by diplomatic missions
1. The provisions of the present Convention apply also, so far as the context permits, to the exercise of consular functions by a diplomatic mission.
2. The names of members of a diplomatic mission assigned to the consular section or otherwise charged with the exercise of the

consular functions of the mission shall be notified to the Ministry for Foreign Affairs of the receiving State or to the authority designated by that Ministry.

3. In the exercise of consular functions a diplomatic mission may address:
(a) the local authorities of the consular district;
(b) the central authorities of the receiving State if this is allowed by the laws, regulations and usages of the receiving State or by relevant international agreements.
4. The privileges and immunities of the members of a diplomatic mission referred to in paragraph 2 of this Article shall continue to be governed by the rules of international law concerning diplomatic relations.

Article 71

Nationals or permanent residents of the receiving State

1. Except in so far as additional facilities, privileges and immunities may be granted by the receiving State, consular officers who are nationals of or permanently resident in the receiving State shall enjoy only immunity from jurisdiction and personal inviolability in respect of official acts performed in the exercise of their functions, and the privilege provided in paragraph 3 of Article 44. So far as these consular officers are concerned, the receiving State shall likewise be bound by the obligation laid down in Article 42. If criminal proceedings are instituted against such a consular officer, the proceedings shall, except when he is under arrest or detention, be conducted in a manner which will hamper the exercise of consular functions as little as possible.
2. Other members of the consular post who are nationals of or permanently resident in the receiving State and members of their families, as well as members of the families of consular officers referred to in paragraph 1 of this Article, shall enjoy facilities, privileges and immunities only in so far as these are granted to them by the receiving State. Those members of the families of members of the consular post and those members of the private staff who are themselves nationals of or permanently resident in the receiving State shall likewise enjoy facilities, privileges and immunities only in so far as these are granted to them by

the receiving State. The receiving State shall, however, exercise its jurisdiction over those persons in such a way as not to hinder unduly the performance of the functions of the consular post.

Article 72
Non-discrimination
1. In the application of the provisions of the present Convention the receiving State shall not discriminate as between States.
2. However, discrimination shall not be regarded as taking place:
(a) where the receiving State applies any of the provisions of the present Convention restrictively because of a restrictive application of that provision to its consular posts in the sending State;
(b) where by custom or agreement States extend to each other more favourable treatment than is required by the provisions of the present Convention.

Article 73
Relationship between the present Convention and other international agreements
1. The provisions of the present Convention shall not affect other international agreements in force as between States parties to them.
2. Nothing in the present Convention shall preclude States from concluding international agreements confirming or supplementing or extending or amplifying the provisions thereof.

Chapter V: Final Provisions
Article 74
Signature
The present Convention shall be open for signature by all States Members of the United Nations or of any of the specialized agencies or Parties to the Statute of the International Court of Justice, and by any other State invited by the General Assembly of the United Nations to become a party to the Convention, as follows until 31 October 1963 at the Federal Ministry for Foreign Affairs of the Republic of Austria and subsequently, until 31 March 1964, at the United Nations Headquarters in New York.

Article 75
Ratification

The present Convention is subject to ratification. The instruments of ratification shall be deposited with the Secretary-General of the United Nations.

Article 76

Accession

The present Convention shall remain open for accession by any State belonging to any of the four categories mentioned in Article 74. The instruments of accession shall be deposited with the Secretary-General of the United Nations.

Article 77
Entry into force

1. The present Convention shall enter into force on the thirtieth day following the date of deposit of the twenty-second instrument of ratification or accession with the Secretary-General of the United Nations.
2. For each State ratifying or acceding to the Convention after the deposit of the twenty-second instrument of ratification or accession, the Convention shall enter into force on the thirtieth day after deposit by such State of its instrument of ratification or accession.

Article 78
Notifications by the Secretary-General

The Secretary-General of the United Nations shall inform all States belonging to any of the four categories mentioned in Article 74:

(a) of signatures to the present Convention and of the deposit of instruments of ratification or accession, in accordance with Articles 74, 75 and 76;

(b) of the date on which the present Convention will enter into force, in accordance with Article 77.

Article 79
Authentic texts
The original of the present Convention, of which the Chinese, English, French, Russian and Spanish texts are equally authentic, shall be deposited with the Secretary-General of the United Nations, who shall send certified copies thereof to all States belonging to any of the four categories mentioned in Article 74.

IN WITNESS WHEREOF the undersigned Plenipotentiaries, being duly authorised thereto by their respective Governments, have signed the present Convention.

DONE AT VIENNA, this twenty-fourth day of April, one thousand nine hundred and sixty-three.

Annex III

Glossary of Diplomatic Terms

Accession
The procedure by which a nation becomes a party to an agreement already in force between other nations.

Accords
International agreement originally thought to be for lesser subjects than covered by treaties, but now really by a different name.

Ad Referendum
An agreement reached ad referendum means an agreement reached by negotiators at the table, subject to the subsequent concurrence of their governments.

Agrément
Diplomatic courtesy requires that before a state appoints a new chief of diplomatic mission to represent it in another state, it must be first ascertained whether the proposed appointee is acceptable to the receiving state. The acquiescence of the receiving State is signified by its granting its Agrément to the appointment. It is unusual for an Agrément to be refused, but it occasionally happens.

Aide Memoir
A written summary of the key points made by a diplomat in an official conversation. Literally, a document left with the other party to the

conversation, either at the time of the conversation or subsequently, as an to memory.

Alternat
When an agreement is signed between two States, or among several States, each signatory keeps an official a copy for itself. Alternat refers to the principle which provides that a State's own name will be listed ahead of the other signatory, or signatories, in its own copy. It is a practice devised centuries ago to handle sensitivities to national pride over precedence.

Ambassador Extraordinary and Plenipotentiary
The Chief of a diplomatic; the ranking official diplomatic representative of his country to the country to which he is accredited, and the personal representative of his own head of State to the head of state of the host country. The term 'extraordinary' has no real meaning. Years ago, it was given only to nonresident ambassadors on temporary missions and was used to distinguish them from regular resident ambassadors. The latter resented others having this appellation, as it seemed to imply a lesser position for themselves. Eventually therefore, it was accorded to them as well. "Plenipotentiary" also comes down through the years. Today it simply means possessed of full powers to do an ambassador's normal job.

Ambassador-designate
An official who has been named to be an ambassador, but who has not yet taken his oath of office.

Asylum
Used in diplomacy to mean the giving of refuge in two senses: first, within the extraterritorial grounds of an embassy (not generally done in American embassy); and the second, when one State allows someone to live within its borders out of the reach of the authority of a second state from which the persons seeks protection.

Attaché
Civilian attaches are junior officers in an embassy or, if more senior, officers who have a professional specialization such as 'labour

attaché", commercial attaches", "cultural attaché" etc. On the military side, an embassy will generally have an army attaché, naval attaché, or air attaché ... and often all three. In American embassies, the senior of the three is called the defense attaché and is in charge of all military attaché activities. These consist largely of liaison work with local military authorities and of keeping informed on host country order of battle.

Bag, The
The DAC refers to the diplomatic 'pouch'. The diplomatic bag enjoys immunity under the Vienna Convention of Diplomatic Relations. The bag day is the day when all mail meant for Headquarters are finalized and dispatched.

Belligerency
A state of belligerency is a state of armed conflict. Belligerents are participants in the conflict.

Bilateral
Bilateral discussions or negotiations are between a state and one other. A bilateral treaty is between one state and one other. "Multilateral" is used when more than two states are involved.

A Bout De Papier
A very informal means of conveying written information; more informal than an aide memoir   or a memorandum.

Breaking Relations
The formal act of severing diplomatic relations with another state to underscore disapproval of its actions or policies. It is generally an unwise step, because when relations between states are most strained is when the maintaining of diplomatic relations is most important. It makes little sense to keep diplomats on the scene when things are going relatively well and then take them aw when they are most needed. An intermediate step which indicates serious displeasure but stops short of an actual diplomatic break is for a government to recall its ambassador indefinitely. This is preferable to a break in relations as his embassy will continue to function, but again this comes

under the heading of cutting one's nose to spite one's face. It a dramatic gesture of this kind is needed, it is far better promptly and publicly to recall an ambassador for consultations, and then just as promptly return him to his post.

Casus Belli
An action by one state regarded as so contrary to the interests of another state as to be considered by that second state as a cause for war.

Chancery
The office was the Chief of Mission and his staff work. This office is often called the embassy, but this is a misnomer. Technically, the embassy is where the ambassador lives, not where he works, although in earlier times, when diplomatic missions were smaller, this was usually the same building. Today, for clarity's sake, many diplomats now distinguish between the two by using the terms 'embassy residence' and 'embassy office'.

Communiqué
A brief public summary statement issued following important bilateral or multilateral meetings. These tend to be bland and full of stock phrases such as 'full and frank discussions", and the like. Occasionally, getting an agreement on the communiqué turns out to be the most difficult part of the meeting.

Conciliation
An effort to achieve agreement and, hopefully, increase goodwill between two opposed parties.

Concordat
A treaty to which the Pope is a party.

Conference or Congress
International meetings. In the diplomatic sense, a Congress has the same meeting as a Conference.

Consular Agent

An official doing consular work for a nation in a locality where it does not maintain a regular Consulate. This official is usually a national of his host state, and his work is usually part-time. (A consular agent is usually distinguished from a consul who, in most cases, is a career diplomat but serving at his country's consular post and for the time being, performing consular functions).

Consulate

An office established by one state in an important city of another state for the purpose of supporting and protecting its citizens traveling or residing there. In addition, these offices are charged with performing other important administrative duties such as issuing visas (where this is required) to host country nationals wishing to travel to the country the consulate represents. All consulates, whether located in the capital city or in other communities, are administratively under the ambassador and the embassy. In addition to carrying out their consular duties, they often serve as branch offices for the embassy, supporting; for example, the latter's political and economic responsibilities. Consulates are expected to play a particularly significant role with the promotion of their own country's exports and other commercial activities. Officers performing consular duties are known as Consuls or, if more junior, vice consuls. The chief of the consulate is known as the Consul or Consul General as in the case of larger Consulates.

Consul Honorary

A host-country national appointed by a foreign state to perform limited consular functions in a locality where the appointing state has no other consular representation.

Convention

An agreement between two or more states, often more, concerning matters of common interest. While supposedly used for lesser matters than embraced in a treaty, it often deals with important subjects indeed—international postal and copyright laws, for example of the law of the sea.

Credentials

The name for the letters given to an ambassador by his Head of State, and addressed to the Head of State of his host country. They are delivered to the latter by ambassadors in a formal credential ceremony, which generally takes place shortly after his arrival at his new post. Until this ceremony has taken place, the host country does not formally recognize him, and he cannot officially act as an ambassador. The letters are termed "Letters of Credence" because they request the receiving Head of State to give "Full credence" to what the ambassador will say on behalf of his government.

Declaration

This can have two quite distinct meanings in diplomacy. It can first, of course, mean a unilateral statement by one state, ranging from an expression of opinion or policy to a declaration of war. It can also mean a joint statement by two or more states having the same binding effect as a treaty. In this latter connection declarations can be put forward either in their own right or appended to a treaty as an added understanding or interpretation.

Delegation

Again used in two senses in diplomacy. "Delegation" can be the term used to refer to the specific powers delegates by his government to a diplomat acting in certain specific circumstances. It also refers to an official party sent to an international conference or on some other special diplomatic mission.

Demarché

An approach, a making of representations. Still very common term used by diplomats to indicate the official raising of a matter with host country officials, often accompanied by a specific request for some type of action or decision in connection with it.

Détente

An easing of tension between States.

Diplomatic Corps

The body of foreign diplomats assembled at a nation's capital. In cities where consuls and consul general are resident, they are collectively known as the consular corps. The dean of both corps is usually that official who had been at his post the longest. There are exceptions to this later rule, however. For example, in some Catholic countries, the papal nuncio is always the dean. The dean represents the corps in collective dealings with host country officials on matters of a ceremonial or administrative character affecting the corps as a whole.

Diplomatic Illness

The practice of feigning illness to avoid participation in a diplomatic event of one kind or another and at the same time to avoid giving formal offense. "Diplomatic deafness" is a somewhat related concept whereby older diplomats allegedly turn this infirmity to advantage by not hearing what they prefer not to hear.

Diplomatic Privileges and Immunities

Historically accorded in recognition that the diplomat represents (and is responsible to) a different sovereignty; also in order that the legitimate pursuit of his official duties will not be impeded in any unnecessary way. They include inviolability of person and premises and exemption from taxation and the civil and criminal jurisdiction of local courts.

Diplomatist

It has the same meaning as "diplomat". An outdated word rarely used now in spoken diplomacy but occasionally still appearing in the literature of diplomacy.

Dispatch

A written, as opposed to a telegraphic, message from an embassy to its home office or vice versa.

Economic Officer

A career diplomat who specialized in economics rather than political, administrative, or other matters.

Embassy
The residence of an ambassador. In recent years, also inaccurately used to denote the building which contains the offices of the ambassador and other key members of his staff. The proper term for the latter, as noted above, is the "chancery". As also noted above, confusion is nowadays avoided through the practice of using the two terms "embassy residence" and "embassy office".

Entente
Denotes a close understanding between certain nations. It suggests mutual and complementary efforts, and a sense of compatible objectives. It can be agreed on orally or in writing, but as a concept is generally less binding than a treaty relationship.

Envoy
Nowadays used to refer to any senior diplomat. Earlier it had a specific hierarchical connotation, being used to designate diplomatic agents of less than the highest rank.

Excellency
An archaic but still much-used title for addressing an ambassador. Theoretically, an American ambassador is not supposed to be addressed this way, but he generally is – along with all his other ambassadorial colleagues. "Mr. Ambassador" is more accurate and less silly. That he is; he may or may not be "excellent."

Exchange of Notes
A common way of recording an agreement. The contents of the notes are, of course, agreed upon in advance by the two nations participating in the exchange.

Exequatur
A document issued to a Consul by the host country government authorizing him to carry out his consular duties.

Ex Gracia
Something which is done as a gesture of good will and not on the basis of an accepted legal obligation.

Extradition

The term for the process, governed by formally concluded agreements, by which fugitives fleeing justice from one country are returned from the country where they have sought refuge. It does not apply to political offenses.

Extraterritoriality

The exercise by one nation, as a result of formally concluded agreements, of certain sovereign functions within the territory of another state. A curtailment of the jurisdiction of the latter state in certain specified areas and/or in certain specified respects.

Final Act (Acte Final)

A formal summary statement, drawn up at the conclusion of a conference.

Foreign Affairs Community

An American government term used to denote the State Department and other government departments and agencies (Defense, Commerce, Agriculture, Treasury, U.S. Information Agency, the Central Intelligence Agency, the Agency for International Development, etc.) which have special interests and responsibilities in the foreign affairs field.

F.S.O.

Shorthand for a career Foreign Service Officer.

Full Powers

A document which authorizes a diplomat to conduct and consummate special business on behalf of his government, such as the settlement of a dispute or the negotiation and signing of a treaty. Before signing a treaty, a diplomat is obligated to show his full-powers document to the other parties involved.

Good Offices

An effort by a third state, or by an individual or an international body, designed to stimulate the processes of settlement in a dispute between two other states.

Guarantee, Treaty of
A treaty which requires signatories to guarantee that situations agreed upon will be maintained. The honoring of such commitments can precipitate armed conflicts.

Legation
These are rare now, but they were once very common. A legation is a diplomatic mission similar for most practical purposes to an embassy, but lower in rank, and presided over by a minister rather than an ambassador. For most of the last century, American diplomatic representation abroad was limited to legations, and for much of this century, the U.S. was represented in more countries by legations than it was by embassies.

Letters of Credence
See Credentials.

Letters of Recall
Also presented by a new ambassador, along with his letter of credence, to the chief of state of his host country during his credentials-presentation ceremony. It is the official document which formally recalls his predecessor.

Protocol
Refers to the ceremonial side of diplomacy, including matters of diplomatic courtesy and precedence.

Protocol
Another name for an agreement. Originally a protocol was considered a somewhat less formal document than a treaty, but that is a distinction no longer valid. A protocol may be an agreement in its own right. It also may constitute added sections which clarify or alter an agreement, or it may be used to add new subjects of agreement to the original document.

Rapporteur
The official of a committee or subcommittee whose jobs is to prepare a summary report of its discussions and conclusions.

Rapprochment
The establishment of improved relations.

Ratification
The act, subsequent to a treaty's having been negotiated, by which a government commits itself to adhere to that treaty. In the United States, it is inaccurate to speak of the Senate's ratifying a treaty. The executive does this, but only after the Senate has given its consent.

Tour D'Horizon
A diplomatic discussion covering most (or at least a number of) subjects of current and common concern.

Treaty
A formal mutually binding agreement between countries. The term comes from *traiter*, to negotiate.

Ultimatum
A last statement indicating a final position. On occasion a prelude to the initiation of military action.

Unfriendly Act
A term used when one government wishes to tell another that an action the latter has taken is regarded as so serious that it might lead to a military action against it. An action which may lead to war.

Visa
Written authority to enter a country for either temporary or permanent residence, depending on its wording.

Adapted from: *http://www.ediplomat.com*

Index

Accession, 63, 68 ,141
Accreditation, 57
Acknowledgement Letters
   - structure of, 2-5
Acting High Commissioner en titre, 59
   - letter of introduction of, 53-54
Adherence, 68
African
   - Heads of States, 24-25
   - Union, 49, 76
Ambassadors
   - and Consuls General
   - appointment of, 23, 27
   - instructions, 77
Appointment
   - of Ambassadors and Consul
      General, 27
   - of a Special Envoy, 27
Authentic texts, 142

Bilateral
   - agreements, 56
   - Political Relations, 64-65
   - relations, 33-34

Career Consular officers
   - Facilities, privileges and
      immunities of, 127-135
Certificate of Exchange, 70
Chancery Report, 3-4
Charge 'd'Affaires
   - ad interim, 51
   - en titre, 51-52, 59,76
Chief of Protocol, 59
Commemoration of National
monument, 31

Commission,   41, 54
Communiques,   63
Completion of General Elections, 31
Concluding Statement, 2, 4
Condolence
   - Letters, 27-31
   - messages
   - concept of time, 28
Conferment of Honours, 31
Congratulatory
   - letter, 32
   - messages 27, 31-36
   - occasions for, 31-32
   - tone of, 27
Consular
   - archives and documents, 123
   - inviolability of, 136-137
   - commission, 115
   - fees and charges, 127
   - functions, 112-114
   - by diplomatic missions, 138-139
   - matters, 66-67
   - officers
   - nationality of, 119
   - posts, 17, 135
   - Relations in General, 111-121
   - staff
   - appointment of, 118
Consulate, 54
Consulate General , 54, 75
Content, 2-4
Corporate objectives, 5
Correspondence
   - between Heads of State, 23-24
   - between officials of Diplomatic
      Missions, 20
   - on arrival at post, 62

- relating to letters of Credence, 39-41
- relating to Letters of invitation, 36-38
- relating to Special Envoys
- characteristics of, 45
- to acknowledge receipt of letters,1
- to forward letters, 5
- in a foreign language, 7-9
- to forward sealed letters, 6
- with attached copy,   6-7
Council Memos, 63
Covering letter, 3, 6
- writing of, 8
Credentials, 39, 43-44, 57, 59
Current Evaluated potential(CEP), 84
Customs duties and inspection
- exemption from, 131-132,137

Diplomatic
- acts, 117
- communication, 39,73-75, 89
- community, 73
- corps, 60-61
- correspondence, 11, 39, 73-75, 89
- functions, 78-79
- mission, 51, 74-79,87-88
- relations, 78
- services, 73, 75
- skills, 86
- systems, 73, 75
- Tasks, 78-79, 82
- tradition, 51
- Value of the occasion, 33
Documents Relating to Treaties, 68-71

Economic
- Community of West African States (ECOWAS), 76
- Relations, 65
- Election
- as Presidential Head of State, 35
- of a new President or Re-election of incumbent, 31
European Union(E.U.), 63-65

Foreign
- Affairs officials, 5
- Diplomatic missions, 29
- Language, 7-8
- policy, 7, 75-77, 89
- Service, 1, 80, 82
- Service Inspection, 80
Formal personal letter, 16
Forwarding
- Correspondence, 10
- Simplified message, 10
- letters, 7, 9
Freedom
- of Communication, 124-125
- of movement, 124
Full Powers, 23, 55-57, 68
- format of, 55-56

Global politics, 74
Globalization, 74
Government
- bureaucracy, 5
- full power, 56-57
G77, 76

Head of official Delegation as special Envoy, 47
Heavily Indebted Countries (HIC), 65
Hosting major international events, 31
Human Resource Development
- quality of, 81
Human Rights, 66

Immigration policy, 47
Immunity from jurisdiction, 128
Inspection System, 80-81
Inter-state relations, 24
International action and sympathy, 28

Joint Communique´, 70-71

La courtoisie,   18

Letter
- of Accreditation, 57-58
- of Appointment Ambassador,41
- of Charge d'*Affaires en titre*, 51-53
- of Consuls General, 51, 54-55
- of full Powers, 51,54-55
- of High Commissioners, 42-43
- of Commission, 41-42
- of Condolence
    - Signed and sealed, 30-31
- transmission of, 29
- of Correspondence
  transmission of, 29
- of Credence, 39-41,43-44,52-53,60-61
- of format of,52
- of Charge d'*Affaires en titre*, 53
- of Recall
- format of, 43-44
- of Recall of Ambassadors, 43-44
- to announce arrival at post, 59-60
- to Announce Assumption of Duty, 60-61
- acknowledgement of, 61
- to introduce a Special Envoy,45-47
- of introduction of Acting High Commissioner *en titre*, 51, 53, 59

Matters of mutual interest
- proposals on, 27
Massages of Congratulation, 31
Memorandum of Understanding on Mutual Cooperation, 64
Mission Action Program, 77, 80
Mode of Communication between Missions, 11
Multilateral
- conference, 56
- institutions, 76
- responsibilities, 76
- treaties, 69

National
- Assembly
- inauguration of, 36

- Day Anniversary, 31,33
- Emergency, 29
    - flag and coat of -arms
- use of, 122
- Monument
- commemoration of, 36
- Tragedy, 27-28
Nigerian
- Foreign policy, 77
- Public Service, 82
Non
- career foreign Ministers and Ambassadors......... 64
- chalance, 2
Note Verbale, 15-17, 21

Obasanjo, Olusegun, 8
Official
- Correspondence, 17, 25
- Letter, 16-21, 24, 26
- format of, 17-20
- when to use, 20-22
- Mail, 6
- Note, 15-16
Opening, 2-3, 12-13
Order of Precedence, 51
Overseas postings, 86

Performance
- Evaluation at headquarters, 80, 86
- Measurement, 73
- framework of, 75
Personal services and contributions
- exemption from, 132,133
Plenipotentiarie, 69
Political Advantage, 47
Pre-Summit Diplomacy
- special envoys in, 48
Presidential
- Correspondence, 25, 36
- body of, 25-26
- closing of, 26
- common forms of, 27-38
- opening of, 24-25
- specialized, 39-58

Preventive Diplomacy
- special envoys in, **47-49**
Private Sector Organization, 5
Privileges and immunities
- waiver of, 129
Proposals on matters of mutual
interest, 27
Public
- Diplomacy, 87
- Relations and Cultural Unit
  (PRCU), 87
- service reform, 74

Quality of
- Leadership in MFA, 79
- relationship of MFAs and Missions,
  79-80
Question of Relevance, 32

Ratification, 68-70, 141
- Instrument of, 69-70
Recruitment and promotion procedures,
81-82
Reference, 12
Regional Organizations, 78
Registration of aliens and residence
permits
- exemption from, 129-130, 137
Reward system for performance
- model of, 83-84
Rules of Procedure, 57

Salutation of Official Letters (l'appel), 18
Sealed envelopes, 6
Semi-Official Correspondence, 16
Signature, 2, 4-5
Simplified Options, 9-10
Social Security Exemption, 130
Special
- Envoys, 45
- appointments of, 23, 27, 73, 89
- feature of, 45
- in a Pre-Summit Diplomacy, 48-49

- in preventive Diplomacy, 47-48
- profile of, 45
- Invitations, 27
Standard
- formats or formulae, 11
- Official Letter, 24
State visit, 15
Substantive Issues, 64
Successful completion of General
Elections, 31

Talking Points, 63-68
- standard format of, 64, 67-68
Taxation
- exemption from, S131, 138
- - of consular premises
- exemption from, 123, 136
Technical Cooperation, 66
Theocratic States, 25
Third Person Notes, 11-17, 29
- common features of, 11-14
- ending of, 13
- identifiable parts, 12-14
- subject – matter of, 13
Tour of duty, 43
Tourism, 48
Tradition, 2
Training and Welfare requirements, 81
Treaty
- definition of, 68

Uniform Standards of performance, 86-
88
United Nations, 76, 91, 107
Unofficial Translation, 7-10

Victory of National Team an
International Competition, 31
Vienna Convention on Diplomatic
Relations, (1961), 91-108,
Vienna Convention on Diplomatic
Relation (1963), 109
Vienna Convention on the Law of
Treaties, 68

Wade, Abdoulaye, 8
Welfare and Performance Measurement, 85
Work permits
- exemption from, 130

Written
- communication, 11, 80, 85
- skill, 79
- correspondence, 2, 24,25
- expression, 1

www.ingramcontent.com/pod-product-compliance
Lightning Source LLC
Chambersburg PA
CBHW021829020426
42334CB00014B/547